京华旧影

Old Photos of Beijing

首都图书馆 编

Edited by the Capital Library of China

学苑出版社

Academy Press

图书在版编目（CIP）数据

京华旧影 / 首都图书馆编 ；王冰译. — 北京 ：学苑出版社，2018.4

ISBN 978-7-5077-5463-6

Ⅰ．①京… Ⅱ．①首… ②王… Ⅲ．①北京－地方史－清后期－摄影集②北京－地方史－民国－摄影集 Ⅳ．①K291-64

中国版本图书馆CIP数据核字（2018）第072752号

翻　　译：王　冰

责任编辑：战葆红
出版发行：学苑出版社
社　　址：北京市丰台区南方庄2号院1号楼
邮政编码：100079
网　　址：www.book001.com
电子信箱：xueyuanpress@163.com
联系电话：010-67601101（营销部）　67603091（总编室）
经　　销：新华书店
印　刷　厂：北京赛文印刷有限公司
开本尺寸：889×1194　1/16
印　　张：16.25
字　　数：160千字
版　　次：2018年8月北京第1版
印　　次：2018年8月第1次印刷
定　　价：580.00元

策　划：肖维平

统　筹：李冠南　　陈　坚

主　编：马文大　　孟云剑

副主编：袁碧荣　　郭　炜　　张小野

编　委：王　琦　　郑春蕾　　李梦楠　　丁小蕾　　张　田
　　　　闫　虹　　程　序　　韩　佳　　张一楠　　陈　飏

翻　译：王　冰

Planner: Xiao Weiping

Coordinators: Li Guannan　　Chen Jian

Editors-in-Chief: Ma Wenda　　Meng Yunjian

Associate Editors-in-Chief: Yuan Birong　　Guo Wei　　Zhang Xiaoye

Editorial Members: Wang Qi　　Zheng Chunlei　　Li Mengnan　　Ding Xiaolei　　Zhang Tian
　　　　　　　　　　　Yan Hong　　Cheng Xu　　Han Jia　　Zhang Yinan　　Chen Yang

Translator: Wang Bing

序 言

　　北京是一座建城 3000 多年、建都 800 多年的历史文化名城。这座城市拥有世界文化遗产 7 处，对外开放的景观达 200 多处，在历史文化遗产的丰富和珍贵程度上令人叹为观止。"城"的辉煌、"都"的风光，名胜古迹的灵气，凝聚成这座城市独一无二的历史底蕴。北京的魅力，固然在山清水秀中，在亭台楼榭间，却也在百姓生活的胡同街巷、市井院落里。然而，北京这座城市巍峨壮丽的城垣宫殿、美轮美奂的苑囿风光、纵横交错的市街坊巷、独具特色的风土人情，在摄影术传入北京前，除了在少数画匠绘笔之下留存之外，大部分都随着岁月的流淌湮没在历史的记忆之中。

　　1839 年，摄影术在法国诞生，很快风靡整个世界。清末，随着外国人大量来华经商传教，摄影术也由此传入中国。1860 年，费利斯·比托作为摄影记者来到北京，他是第一位到中国北方和北京拍照的西方摄影师。自此以后，许多身份各异、目的不同的外国人（如约翰·汤姆逊、甘博等）陆续来到北京，拿起照相机拍摄了大量照片，为北京留下了许多弥足珍贵的历史影像。随着摄影术的传入，本土的照相馆也应运而生。1892 年，任庆泰在琉璃厂创办了丰泰照相馆，这是北京最早的照相馆。摄影术在中国崭露头角之后，主要用于新闻或工程纪事，在形象地反映现实生活和记录新鲜事物方面，可谓独树一帜，受到了朝廷的重视和官民的欢迎。1909 年，在修建京张铁路时，詹天佑就曾委托同生照相馆的谭景堂拍摄《京张路工撮影》。随着摄影术的逐渐普及，越来越多的内容被摄入镜头，巍巍古城、悠悠小巷、达官贵人、贩夫走卒、风俗民情、社会生活等诸多片段永远地被定格在那个时代，其内容之广泛，时间跨度之长，令人惊叹不已。

世易时移，昔日的城垣古韵和市井生活大多已经消逝，但历史不可割断，这些照片已成为当今研究北京历史文化的重要文献，具有很高的学术价值和史料价值。首都图书馆藏有反映北京历史文化的老照片 1.4 万余幅。为满足业务交流和文献资源共享的需求，首都图书馆精选出其中的 239 幅，整理成册，配以说明文字，推出了《京华旧影》图片集。此图片集从城垣古韵、街衢巷陌、风俗节令、坐贾行商、市井生活、交通运输 6 个方面，采用图文并茂的形式，向读者展现消失的社会生活和文化景观。

2017 年 8 月，在推进全国文化中心建设领导小组第一次会议上，北京市市委书记蔡奇强调，要建设全国文化中心、要把北京建设成为弘扬中华文明与引领时代潮流的文化名城、中国特色社会主义先进文化之都。为落实北京市委、市政府建设全国文化中心工作要求，进一步挖掘北京的历史文化内涵，首都图书馆根据北京市文化建设要重点抓好"一核一城三带两区"的要求，对馆藏 1.4 万余幅反映北京历史文化的老照片重新做了梳理，精选出长城摊贩、通惠河、御河、高粱桥等有关三个文化带的老照片，加入到《京华旧影》中。在首都文化建设的新形势下，在丰富内容、修订图文的基础上，首都图书馆推出一批珍贵的影像资料，这既是对历史文化的保护，又可加强民众对北京作为历史文化名城的了解，对于建设全国文化中心至为重要。

北京是一部历史巨著，其独特的魅力贯穿古今；北京是一幅时光画卷，传统在这里延续，现代在这里辉煌。新时代，北京正昂首阔步走向未来，她的画卷会越来越美，越来越丰富多彩！我们衷心祝愿读者在品读《京华旧影》时，鉴古知今，古为今用，在欣赏中发现北京的美，感受北京的韵味。

编者
2017 年 12 月

Preface

Built over 3000 years ago and made capital over 800 years ago, Beijing is a famous historic and cultural city, home to seven sites in the list of World Cultural Heritage and more than 200 scenic spots open to the public. The richness and preciousness of its historical and cultural heritage are beyond our imagination. The glory of the city, the scenery of the capital, and the spirit of the historical sites in combination have become the unique charm of this city. Its glamour exists not only in the refreshing natural scenery and fanciful pavilions but also in the citizens' everyday life in hutongs and courtyards. Beijing boasts imposing city walls and palaces, crisscrossed streets and unique culture. Before photography was introduced to Beijing, most of the images here were forgotten except a few recorded by painters.

Photography, invented in 1839 in France, has since spread to the world. At the end of the Qing Dynasty (1644-1911), when many foreigners came to China for missionary and business reasons, it was also brought to China. In 1860, a cameraman called Felice Beato came to China as the first western photographer who shot northern China including the capital city. Since then, many foreigners (like John Thmson and Sidney D. Gamble) with different capacities and purposes came to Beijing and took many precious pictures which recorded the history of the city. Local photo studios also appeared as photography was introduced, with the first one—the Fengtai Photo Studio, opening on Glass Street in 1892 by Ren Qingtai. After it was initially used for press and recording projects, photography was given great importance by the royal court and was popular among people thanks to its objective reflection of real life and its function of recording novel things. For example, Tan Jingtang from Tongsheng Photo Studio, was invited by Zhan Tianyou, a famous railway engineer, to take pictures of workers building the Beijing-Zhangjiakou Railway in 1909. As the popularity of photography grew, more things were recorded by cameras, including ancient cities, quiet alleys, high officials, peddlers and servants, customs and social life, with an astonishingly wide coverage and long time span.

While ancient cities and the life of ordinary persons in the past have disappeared as time goes by, these pictures have become important resources for studying the history and culture of Beijing, with both rich academic and historical value because history never stops. In order to meet the demand of business-exchange and literature resource-sharing, the Capital Library has chosen 239 photos among the over 14,000 old pictures reflecting Beijing's history and culture to compile the album, Old Photos of Beijing, with explanations for each one, including: the ancient city walls, streets and lanes, customs and festivals, shops and venders, the daily life of ordinary people and traffic. This album showcases the bygone social life and culture of the capital city.

At the first meeting of the Leading Group for Building Beijing into the National Cultural Center in August 2017, Cai Qi, the Secretary the CPC Committee of Beijing, emphasized the importance of building Beijing into a national cultural center and a famous cultural city, carrying forward Chinese civilization on one hand and leading the times on the other, and to showcase Socialism with Chinese characteristics. In order to implement the requirements of the CPC Committee and the government of Beijing, to find more historical and cultural essence of Beijing, and to meet the standards for strengthening culture in the city, the Capital Library has selected for the album old photos from three cultural circles, like the peddlers on the Great Wall, the Tonghuihe River, and the moat and the Gaoliang Bridge, among the 14,000 photos reflecting Beijing's history and culture. Against the background of a developing culture in the capital, the Library has published these valuable photos after editing and revising both pictures and illustrations, which will help protect Beijing's history and culture, enable people to know more about Beijing, It's very important to build the city into the national cultural center.

Beijing is a historical masterpiece with its unique glamour shining both in the past and at present; Beijing is a scroll painting of time where tradition is carried forward and modern times find its glory. In the new era, the city is striding toward an even more colorful and diverse future. We sincerely hope that readers learn from the past, cherish the present, and learn to appreciate the beauty and charm of Beijing while enjoying this album.

Editor
December 2017

目 录
Contents

城垣古韵   1
Ancient City Walls

街衢巷陌   55
Streets and Lanes

风俗节令   87
Customs and Festivals

坐贾行商   123
Shops and Vendors

市井生活   175
The Daily Life of Ordinary People

交通运输   207
Traffic

主要摄影者简介   245
Profile of Major Photographers   247

后记   249
Postscript   250

城垣古韵

Ancient City Walls

紫禁城
The Forbidden City

[德国] 赫达·莫里逊 [Germany] Hedda Morrison

由景山向南所看到的紫禁城。

View of the Forbidden City from the Jingshan on the north.

城垣古韵　　Ancient City Walls

天安门
Tian'anmen

[日本] 小川一真 [Japan] Kazuma Ogawa

天安门是皇城正门，位于皇城南垣正中，始建于明永乐十五年（1417），原名"承天门"。明英宗天顺元年（1457）焚毁，9年后由工部尚书白圭主持重修，基本上具有了现在天安门的规模。门前立有汉白玉华表。天安门是明清两代帝王从事重要活动的地方之一。

Tian'anmen was the front gate of the Imperial City, located in the very centre of the south wall. Built in the 15th year of Yong Le (1417), it was originally named Chengtianmen. Destroyed by fire in the first year of Tian Shun (1457), the gate was restored nine years later with the direction of Bai Gui, the Minister of Works. Two Huabiao columns carved out of white marble were erected in front of it. Tian'anmen served as one of the important places for imperial activities during Ming and Qing Dynasties (1368-1644, 1644-1911).

[美国] 赫伯特·C·怀特 [America] Herbert C. White

佚名 Unknown Photographer

地安门
Di'anmen

地安门是皇城北门，位于皇城北垣正中，南对景山，北对鼓楼，俗称"后门"。建筑形制与西安门类似。1900年八国联军侵入北京后，慈禧太后就是出地安门，再出德胜门远逃西安。1955年2月，为便利城区交通将其拆除。

Di'anmen was the north gate of the Imperial City, located in the very centre of the north wall. It faced southward the Jingshan, northward the Drum Tower, commonly referred to as "back door". Its architectural shape was similar to the Xi'anmen. When the Eight-Power Allied Forces invaded Beijing in 1900, the Empress Dowager Cixi fled to Xi'an through Di'anmen and then passing through the Deshengmen. The gate was removed for traffic convenience in February 1955.

东安门
Dong'anmen

[日本] 小川一真 [Japan] Kazuma Ogawa

东安门位于皇城东垣中间偏南，始建于明永乐十五年（1417）。此照为民国初期自东向西拍摄，透过正中门看到的远处建筑为东华门。1912年，东安门在"北京兵变"中被焚毁。

Dong'anmen, built in the 15th year of Yong Le (1417), was located slightly south in the middle section of the east wall of the Imperial City. The photo was taken in the early period of the Republic of China (1912-1949) from the east. Through the middle door, Donghuamen could be seen in the far distance. It was destroyed by fire during Beijing Mutiny in 1912.

西安门
Xi'anmen

[日本] 小川一真 [Japan] Kazuma Ogawa

西安门位于皇城西垣中段偏北，始建于明永乐十五年（1417）。1900年八国联军入侵后，其南侧的民宅皆毁于战火。1951年因火灾，西安门被焚毁。

Xi'anmen, built in the 15th year of Yong Le (1417), was located slightly north in the middle section of the West wall of the Imperial City. Houses in the south were burnt down after the Eight-Power Allied Forces invaded Beijing in 1900. A conflagration destroyed the Xi'anmen in 1951.

正阳门全景（改造前）
Panorama of Zhengyangmen (Before Reconstruction)

正阳门位于北京内城南垣正中，是明清两代北京城的正门，俗称前门，也是北京城最知名的标志性建筑之一。

Zhengyangmen was located at the very centre of the southern wall of the Inner City of Beijing, serving as the capital's main gate in Ming and Qing Dynasties (1368-1644, 1644-1911). Commonly known as Qianmen (front gate), it was also one of the most well-known landmark buildings in Beijing.

城垣古韵　　Ancient City Walls

佚名 Unknown Photographer

正阳门城楼新开门洞
New Gateways were Opened at Zhengyangmen

1915年，为缓解城市交通，民国政府启动了正阳门改建工程。改造方案由德国建筑师罗克格·凯尔设计。拆除了瓮城及东西闸楼，使原来封闭的瓮城变成了一个开放的空间。

In 1915, the government of the Republic of China started the reconstruction of Zhengyangmen to ease traffic congestion. The reconstruction plans were designed by German architect Rothkegel Kael who removed the barbican ("jar walls", walled enclosure for defense as a trap for the invading enemy) and the lock gates on the east and west side, changed this area into an open place.

佚名 Unknown Photographer

正阳门城楼
Gate Tower of Zhengyangmen

[美国] 西德尼·D·甘博 [America] Sidney D. Gamble

正阳门箭楼
Watchtower of Zhengyangmen

[德国] 海因茨·冯·佩克哈默 [Germany] Heinz v. Perckhammer

此照为改造后的正阳门箭楼，增加了西洋样式的窗洞券套和端墙装饰。

The photo shows the watchtower of the Zhengyangmen after the reconstruction, in which western arched ornaments were added above the windows and at the headwalls.

正阳门箭楼（改造后）
Watchtower of Zhengyangmen (After Reconstruction)

[美国] 赫伯特·C·怀特 [America] Herbert C. White

城垣古韵　　　Ancient City Walls

崇文门
Chongwenmen

[瑞典] 奥斯伍尔德·喜仁龙 [Sweden] Osvald Siren

崇文门位于北京内城南垣东侧，是内外城交通的孔道之一。此照摄于 1921 年，在城楼南面。1901 年为把火车从永定门外马家堡引到城内，八国联军中的英军打通瓮城东西墙，使火车穿城而过。照片是人们在道口等候火车通过的情景。

Chongwenmen was located at the east side of the southern wall of the Inner City, serving as one of the thoroughfares between the Inner and Outer City. The photo was taken in 1921 at the south side of the gate tower. To extend the railway from Majiapu outside Yongdingmen into the city, English soldiers who joined the Eight-Power Allied Forces broke through the east and west walls of the barbican in 1901. The photo shows people waiting at a crossing when a train passed.

南城墙外景
Scenery Outside the South City Wall

［瑞典］奥斯伍尔德·喜仁龙 [Sweden] Osvald Siren

此照为内城南城墙的一段及外城的民居、煤栈。位于前门与宣武门之间。城墙向外突出来的部分叫做墩台，又称马面，呈方形或矩形，三面突出于城墙之外。墩台的平均间距在90米以内，即在弓矢投石的有效射程以内，其作用在于分散来犯之敌的有效兵力，并对城下敌军形成交叉火力，是增强对外防御能力的城防设施。

The photo shows a section of the southern wall of the Inner City, and the folk houses and coal bunkers in the Outer City between Qianmen and Xuanwumen. The square or rectangular shaped parts with three sides protruding from the city wall are called piers or horsefaces. The average distance between these piers lies within 90 meters, which can be covered by shooting arrows and catapulting stones. Therefore, they served as an effective means to disperse enemies, thanks to crossfire from both sides. They were facilities to enhanced defensive strength of the city.

宣武门
Xuanwumen

[瑞典] 奥斯伍尔德·喜仁龙 [Sweden] Osvald Siren

宣武门位于北京内城南垣西侧，与崇文门遥相呼应。此照为1921年从箭楼向北拍摄的城楼全景。瓮城内堆满杂物和建筑材料。

Located at the west side of the southern wall of the Inner City, Xuanwumen sat symmetrically with Chongwenmen. The photo was taken in 1921 from the watchtower in the south, showing a panorama of the gate tower of Xuanwumen. We can see the barbican was full with many sorts of things such as construction materials.

阜成门
Fuchengmen

[瑞典] 奥斯伍尔德·喜仁龙 [Sweden] Osvald Sirén

阜成门位于北京内城西垣南侧。元明清三代，自门头沟开采的煤都要经阜成门进入京城，故有"煤门"之称。为此，城门券洞内曾镌刻一枝梅花，称为"阜成梅花"。此照为20世纪20年代初从西南向东北方向拍摄。

Located at the south side of the west wall of the Inner City, Fuchengmen was the gate, through which, all of the coal mined at Mentougou was transported into the city in the Yuan, Ming and Qing Dynasties (1271-1368, 1368-1644, 1644-1911). With a nickname of "coalgate", the gate featured a plum blossom carved out on wall of the inside arch (as a play on words, in Chinese plum (mei) is homophone to coal mei). The photo was taken in the early 1920s from the southwest.

阜成门外
Outside of Fuchengmen

[瑞典] 奥斯伍尔德·喜仁龙 [Sweden] Osvald Siren

从阜成门箭楼上向外拍摄的景色,城墙马面连绵伸展向远方。

Taken from the watchtower of Fuchengmen, the photo shows the horsefaces in the city wall and their sinuous winding extending into the far distance.

西直门城楼
Gate Tower of Xizhimen

西直门位于北京内城西垣北端。由于清代皇宫的饮用水来自京西玉泉山，通过西直门运进皇宫，故京城百姓将西直门称为"水门"。1969年，因修建北京地铁，西直门被拆除。

Xizhimen was located at the northern end of the western wall of the Inner City. In the Qing Dynasty (1644-1911), drinking water was transported from the Yuquan Mountain in the west of Beijing to the Palace through Xizhimen. Called by the ordinary people as "water gate", it was removed in 1969 due to the construction of the Beijing subway.

[瑞典] 奥斯伍尔德·喜仁龙 [Sweden] Osvald Siren

西直门南侧外景
Scenery at South Side of Xizhimen

图为20世纪20年代初期的西直门城楼、瓮城和箭楼。护城河绕过方方正正的瓮城，自北向南流淌。明末，李自成经由此门进入北京城。清代皇帝去圆明园、颐和园等西郊的御苑皆经此门。

The photo shows the gate tower, barbican and watchtower of Xizhimen in the early 1920s. The city moat bypasses the square, shaped barbican running south. At the end of the Ming Dynasty (1368-1644), Li Zicheng entered Beijing through this gate. When the emperors of the Qing Dynasty (1644-1911) visited the imperial gardens like the Winter Palace or the Summer Palace at the western outskirt, they also passed through here.

[瑞典] 奥斯伍尔德·喜仁龙 [Sweden] Osvald Sirén

德胜门箭楼
Watchtower of Deshengmen

[瑞典] 奥斯伍尔德·喜仁龙 [Sweden] Osvald Sirén

德胜门位于内城北垣西侧，取"旗开得胜"的吉利寓意，明清两代大军出征都出此门。1915年为修环城铁路拆掉瓮城，1921年拆除城楼，所幸箭楼保存至今，建为一座小型博物馆。

Deshengmen ("Gate of Virtuous Victory") was located at the west side of the northern wall of the Inner City, with an implied auspicious meaning of "Raising the banner and gaining victory". In the Ming and Qing Dynasties (1368-1644, 1644-1911), all troops went out to battle by passing through this gate. In 1915, its barbican was removed due to the construction of the Railway circulating the Capital. Leaving the gate tower which was torn down in 1921, the watchtower was fortunately preserved until today and renovated with a little museum inside.

安定门
Andingmen

[日本] 小川一真 [Japan] Kazuma Ogawa

安定门位于内城北垣东侧，始建于明永乐七年（1409）。明清时，无论是抵御还是征讨的军事，回师必由安定门进城。民国初年修环城铁路时拆掉了瓮城，1969年修地铁时拆除城楼、箭楼。

Built in the 7th year of Yong Le (1409), Andingmen was located at the east side of the Inner City's north wall. In the Ming and Qing Dynasties (1368-1644, 1644-1911), the troops of defense or punitive expeditions returned through Andingmen to the city. In the early period of the Republic of China (1912-1949), the barbican was removed due to the construction of the railway circulating the Capital. In 1969, the gate tower and watchtower were torn down due to the subway construction.

安定门箭楼
Watchtower of Andingmen

佚名 Unknown Photographer

民国年间的安定门箭楼。

The watchtower of Andingmen in the period of the Republic of China (1912-1949).

东直门
Dongzhimen

[日本] 小川一真 [Japan] Kazuma Ogawa

东直门位于内城东垣北侧，原址为元大都崇仁门，多走运木料的车，俗称"木门"。北京内外城门的瓮城均为外侧抹角转折的圆弧形平面，唯有东直门与西直门的瓮城为方形平面，直角转折。瓮城南面辟有闸楼、券门。1969年为修地铁拆除东直门城楼。

Built on the site of Chongrenmen of the Yuan Dynasty (1271-1368), Dongzhimen was located at the north part of the eastern wall of the Inner City. Because a lot of carriages transporting timbers passed through, the gate was commonly referred to as "wood gate". The barbicans of the Inner and Outer City of Beijing all used to be in curve shaped without any coigns, but the barbicans of Dongzhimen and Xizhimen were of square shape with right-angle corners. With lock gates and arched gateways south of the barbicans, the gate tower was removed due to subway construction in 1969.

东直门以东城墙
City Wall East of Dongzhimen

[瑞典] 奥斯伍尔德·喜仁龙 [Sweden] Osvald Sirén

20世纪20年代初，在内城东城墙内东直门南顺城街上，从西南向东北方向拍摄的东直门以南的东城墙内壁，墙体显得较平整，似乎是刚修缮不久。

This photo taken from the southwest shows the inner surface of the wall south of Dongzhimen, along the street, next to the wall in the early 1920s. The wall surface seemed to be quite smooth as if it was recently renovated.

朝阳门城楼
Gate Tower of Chaoyangmen

[瑞典] 奥斯伍尔德·喜仁龙 [Sweden] Osvald Sirén

朝阳门位于内城东垣南侧。原城楼、箭楼形制与崇文门相似，朝阳门离通惠河很近，漕粮都由此门入城，存放在朝阳门内的几座大仓库内。也正因如此，朝阳门的标志是瓮城门洞上所刻的一枝谷穗。此照是20世纪20年代初期在城内从西北向东南拍摄的朝阳门城楼北侧面、西侧面。

Located at the south part of the eastern wall of the Inner City, Chaoyangmen features a watchtower and gate tower similar to those of Chongwenmen. Not far from the Tonghuihe, it was the gateway through which tribute rice was transported into the city before being stored in several huge storehouses nearby. Therefore, its symbol was a grain spike carved at the gateway of its barbican. The photo taken from northwest inside the city in the early 1920s shows the north and west surface of its gate tower.

朝阳门外景
Scenery Outside of Chaoyangmen

朝阳门城楼、箭楼、瓮城。1900 年朝阳门箭楼被日军火炮击毁，1903 年重建。1915 年修建环城铁路时拆除瓮城。1953 年拆除城楼及其城台。1958 年拆除箭楼。

The photo shows the gate tower, watchtower, barbican of Chaoyangmen. Destroyed in the Japanese bombardment in 1900, the watchtower was rebuilt in 1903. Due to the construction of the railway circulating the Capital, the barbican was torn down in 1915, the gate tower and wall platform in 1953, and the watchtower in 1958.

[日本] 小川一真 [Japan] Kazuma Ogawa

城垣古韵　　Ancient City Walls

内城西南角楼
Southwestern Corner Tower of the Inner City

[瑞典] 奥斯伍尔德·喜仁龙 [Sweden] Osvald Siren

内城西南角楼位于内城南垣西端与西垣南端交汇处，建于明正统元年至四年（1436—1439）。明清两代多有修葺，但清末失于修缮，至1920年楼顶已残破不堪，于20世纪30年代拆除了角楼，1969年拆除残余墩台。

The southwestern corner tower of the Inner City links the southern wall and west wall. It was built from the 1st year to the 4th year of Zheng Tong (1436 -1439), it underwent several renovations in the Ming and Qing Dynasties (1368 -1644, 1644-1911). Unfortunately, the roof was dilapidated by 1920 due to a lack of repair at the end of the Qing Dynasty. The corner tower was torn down in the 1930s, as were the remnants of the pier in 1969.

内城东南角楼
Southeastern Corner Tower of the Inner City

[瑞典] 奥斯伍尔德·喜仁龙 [Sweden] Osvald Siren

内城东南角楼始建于明正统年间（1436—1449）。明嘉靖年间（1522—1566）在内城以南修建了外城，外城东、西两侧的城墙转接至内城的东、西角楼附近。东南角楼保存至今，是明城墙遗址公园的一部分。

Southeastern corner tower of the Inner City was built in the time of Zheng Tong (1436-1449) and the Outer City in the time of Jia Jing (1522-1566). South to the Inner City, the latter links the Inner City through both its east and west walls near the eastern and western corner towers. The southeastern corner tower has been preserved, as a part of the Ming Dynasty City Wall Relics Park.

永定门外景
Scenery Outside of Yongdingmen

[英国] 唐纳德·曼尼 [Britain] Donald Mennie

永定门是北京外城的正门，是外城规制最大的城门，也是北京城南北中轴线的南端起点。城门上建有门楼，为了不使城门直接暴露在敌人的攻击下，在城门外侧附建瓮城和箭楼，围成一个面积不大的防御性附郭。城墙外面挖有护城河，遇到敌军攻城，则紧闭城门，由箭楼和城墙上的垛口向外射击。永定门城楼与附郭曾于1957年被拆除，2004年于原址重建城楼。

As the biggest city gates in the outer city of old Beijing, Yongdingmen serves as the main gate of the Outer City and also the southern starting point of the north-south axis of Beijing. To avoid exposing the city gate directly to the attacks of enemies, a tower was constructed at the top of the gate, and a barbican and watchtower were added outside, forming a small defensive enclosure. Outside the city wall, the city moat was excavated. In case of an attack, the city gate was closed immediately and arrows shot across the moat from the watchtower and the crenellation on the top of the wall. The gate tower and the outer enclosure were demolished in 1957, but the gate tower was reconstructed at its original place in 2004.

永定门城楼
Gate Tower of Yongdingmen

永定门城楼上两层楼檐间悬挂一块木质匾额，上书"永定门"三字。1957年城楼拆除后，此匾存于首都博物馆。此照为从永定门内拍摄的城楼北侧面。

A wooden plaque was hanged between the two eaves at the top of the tower, inscribed with the three characters "Yongdingmen". It was moved to the Capital Museum in 1957 when the gate tower was demolished. The photo shows the north side of the gate tower.

[瑞典] 奥斯伍尔德·喜仁龙 [Sweden] Osvald Siren

右安门
Youanmen

[瑞典] 奥斯伍尔德·喜仁龙 [Sweden] Osvald Siren

右安门位于外城南垣西侧，城门坐北朝南，与左安门东西相望，又名"南西门"。明嘉靖三十二年（1553）修外城，右安门为外城七门之一。嘉靖四十一年（1562）加筑瓮城。20世纪50年代拆除右安门。此照由南向北拍摄箭楼南侧面，透过箭楼门洞可见城楼门洞。

Located at the western side of the southern wall of the Outer City, the gate faced southward and sat symmetrically on both sides of the city axis with Zuoanmen. Also named as Nanximen, it was one of the seven gates outside when the Outer City was constructed in the 32nd year of Jia Jing (1553). A barbican was built in the 41st year of Jia Jing (1562), but the whole gate tower was demolished in the 1950s. The photo shows the south side of the watchtower. Through the gateway of the watchtower, the gateway of the city could be seen in the distance.

广安门
Guang'anmen

[瑞典] 奥斯伍尔德·喜仁龙 [Sweden] Osvald Siren

广安门位于外城西垣正中偏北，明代名"广宁门"，清代避道光皇帝"宁"之讳，改名"广安门"。始建于明嘉靖三十二年（1553），箭楼为清乾隆十五年（1750）后增建。箭楼及瓮城于20世纪40年代初拆除，1957年拆除城楼。此照系20世纪20年代初在城外从西向东拍摄的箭楼西侧面。

Located slightly north of the mid-point of the western wall of the Outer City, Guang'anmen was named "Guangningmen" in the Ming Dynasty (1368-1644). To avoid the taboo "ning" which appeared in the name of Emperor Daoguang (whose name was min ning) of the Qing Dynasty, the gate name was renamed to its present one. Built in the 32nd year of Jia Jing (1553), the gate tower was demolished in 1957. The watchtower which was added in the 15th year of Qian Long (1750) was broken down in the 1940s together with the barbican. The photo taken in the 1920s showed the west side of the watchtower.

西便门附近角楼
Corner Tower Close to Xibianmen

绿柳掩映下的内城西南角楼，又窄又浅的护城河上横跨一座小木桥，一个男子光着上身在河边担水，共同构成一幅老北京风情画卷。

The southwestern corner tower of Inner City was enclosed by green willows, with a small wooden bridge over the narrow and shallow city moat, and a bare-chested man carrying water, forming a picturesque scenery of old Beijing.

[美国] 赫伯特·C·怀特 [America] Herbert C. White

东便门
Dongbianmen

[瑞典] 奥斯伍尔德·喜仁龙 [Sweden] Osvald Siren

东便门位于外城北垣东段偏西,明清北京城"凸"字形平面的右肩部,建成于明嘉靖三十二年(1553)。此照在城外由北向南拍摄,照片中所见的东便门箭楼和瓮城在北京城门瓮城中是最小的。

Built in the 32nd year of Jia Jing (1553), Dongbianmen was located west of the eastern section of the northern wall of the Outer City, the upper right corner of the Inner City in the Ming and Qing Dynasties (1368-1644,1644-1911). The photo taken in the north outside the city shows the watchtower and barbican, the smallest among all enclosures of its kind in Beijing.

城垣古韵　　Ancient City Walls

东便门外护城河
Moat Outside of Dongbianmen

远处的城楼是北京内城的东南角楼，左侧稍低的城墙即为外城东便门两侧的一段城墙。水面为护城河，也是通向通州的通惠河的终点。护城河从内城西北角分几路环城流淌，最终全部汇流到这里，所以水面较宽，水道深至可以行船。

The gate tower in the distance was the southeastern corner tower of the Inner City, linked to its left with Dongbianmen of the Outer City through a section of the lower wall. The tower was protected by moat which was the end point of Tonghuihe leading to Tongzhou. Joined by the water of other moats starting from the northwest corner of the Inner City, the moat is so wide and deep that boats could pass through.

[德国] 海因茨·冯·佩克哈默 [Germany] Heinz v. Perckhammer

城垣古韵　　Ancient City Walls

广渠门
Guangqumen

广渠门位于外城东垣正中偏北，俗称"沙窝门"。此照是20世纪20年代初在城外从南向北拍摄的广渠门城楼、瓮城、箭楼的南侧面。广渠门虽在建筑形制上比较低矮，但在历史上很有名。明崇祯二年（1629）袁崇焕率军与八旗兵激战于广渠门外，取得保卫京师的广渠门大捷。1917年为纪念他，在广渠门内南侧的龙潭湖畔修建袁督师庙，该庙至今尚存。

Commonly referred to as "Shawomen", Guangqumen was located in slightly north of the mid-point of the eastern wall of the Outer City. The photo taken in the early 1920s shows the south side of the gate tower, barbican and watchtower. Although it was low, it was very famous in history for a fierce defense battle outside the gate in the second year of Chong Zhen (1629), when commander Yuan Chonghuan defeated the Eight Flag soldiers. A temple was built on the riverbanks of Longtan Lake in the south near Guangqumen in 1917, to commemorate him. It still exists today.

[瑞典] 奥斯伍尔德·喜仁龙 [Sweden] Osvald Siren

城垣古韵　　Ancient City Walls

广渠门
Guangqumen

[瑞典] 奥斯伍尔德·喜仁龙 [Sweden] Osvald Sirén

20 世纪 20 年代初在城内从西向东拍摄的广渠门城楼西侧面。城楼拆除于 20 世纪 30 年代。

The photo taken in the early 1920s inside the city shows the west side of the gate tower which was demolished in the 1930s.

左安门
Zuoanmen

[瑞典] 奥斯伍尔德·喜仁龙 [Sweden] Osvald Siren

左安门位于外城南垣东侧，与右安门东西相对，俗称"江擦门"，始建于明嘉靖三十二年（1553），1953年全部拆除。此照为20世纪20年代初，在城门洞内从北向南拍摄的左安门箭楼北侧面。

Located at the east section of the southern wall of the Outer City, Zuoanmen sat symmetrically with You'anmen on both sides of the axis. Built in the 32nd year of Jia Jing (1553) and completely demolished in 1953, it was commonly called "Jiangcamen". The photo taken in the early 1920s shows the north side of the watchtower.

外城西南角楼
Southwestern Corner Tower of the Outer City

外城西南角楼位于外城南垣西端与西垣南端交汇处，1953 年拆除。此照摄于 20 世纪 20 年代初，角楼倒映在清澈的护城河水面上。

Removed in 1953, the southwestern corner tower linked the southern wall and western wall of the Outer City. The photo taken in the early 1920s shows the corner tower mirrored in the clear water of the moat.

[瑞典] 奥斯伍尔德·喜仁龙 [Sweden] Osvald Sirén

外城西北角楼
Northwestern Corner Tower of the Outer City

[瑞典] 奥斯伍尔德·喜仁龙 [Sweden] Osvald Sirén

外城的西北角楼位于外城西垣北端与北垣西端交汇处，建于明嘉靖三十二年（1553），1957年8月拆除。此照摄于20世纪20年代外城北城墙外，远处突出于城墙的建筑是西便门的箭楼、瓮城、城楼。

Built in the 32nd year of Jia Jing (1553) and removed in August 1957, the northwestern corner tower linked the western and northern walls of the Outer City. The photo taken in the 1920s outside the northern wall shows the watchtower, barbican and gate tower of Xibianmen, which were on the wall in the distance.

外城东北角楼残迹
Remains of Northeastern Corner Tower of the Outer City

[瑞典]奥斯伍尔德·喜仁龙 [Sweden] Osvald Siren

外城东北角楼位于外城北垣东端与东垣北端交汇处，1900年八国联军的炮火曾毁坏该角楼，20世纪30年代修建铁路时，角楼城台也被拆除。此照当摄于20世纪20年代，画面中角楼已无存，城台还在。

Linking the northern and eastern walls, the northeastern corner tower of the Outer City was destroyed in artillery bombardment by the Eight-Power Allied Forces in 1900. Its base was removed in the 1930s due to railway construction. The photo taken in the 1920s shows the base without a corner tower.

城墙和护城河
City Wall and Moat

[美国] 西德尼·D·甘博 [America] Sidney D. Gamble

北京除皇城外，宫城、内城、外城均以护城河环绕，于城市内外形成一个整体的水系网。这是20世纪20年代的内城护城河水面。

The city moat is a water system surrounding the Palace City, Inner City and Outer City with the exception of the Imperial City. This was the city moat of the Inner City in the 1920s.

封冻的护城河
The Frozen City Moat

[德国] 赫达·莫里逊 [Germany] Hedda Morrison

鼓楼地区鸟瞰图
Aerial View of the Drum Tower Area

佚名 Unknown Photographer

钟楼、鼓楼位于地安门外大街北端，是北京城中轴线北端的一组标志性建筑。两楼南北纵置，相距百米，鼓楼在南，钟楼在北，气势雄伟，巍峨壮观。曾是明清两代都城的报时中心，更是封建帝王一统江山、皇权永固的象征。

Located at the north end of Di'anmenwai Street, the Bell Tower and the Drum Tower are landmark architecture at the north end of Beijing's central axis. The Bell Tower sits 100 meters north to the Drum Tower. The tall and majestic towers were the centre for the announcement of time during the Ming and Qing Dynasties (1368-1644,1644-1911), symbolizing the rulers' supremacy and their everlasting power.

鼓楼
Drum Tower

[英国] 唐纳德·曼尼 [Britain] Donald Mennie

鼓楼所在位置原系元代大都城的齐政楼，明永乐十八年（1420）重建为鼓楼。鼓楼台基高达 4 米，台上为 5 间重檐木构殿楼，上置巨大的更鼓 24 面。

The Drum Tower was built in the 18th year of Yong Le (1420) on the site of Qizheng Tower in the Yuan Dynasty (1271-1368). With 4-meter-high base, a five-room wooden building with multiple eaves was built, housing 24 large drums to announce time.

钟楼
Bell Tower

[德国] 赫达·莫里逊 [Germany] Hedda Morrison

钟楼在鼓楼以北 100 多米处，原是元代万宁寺的中心阁，始建于至元九年（1272），后来毁于战火。明永乐十八年（1420）与鼓楼一起重建，但不久后就再次被毁。清乾隆十年（1745）奉旨重建，两年后竣工。这次为了防止火灾，建筑全部采用了砖石结构。

Located 100 meters north of Drum Tower, the Bell Tower was built in the 9th year of Zhi Yuan (1272) on the site of the central Tower of the Wanning Temple in the Yuan Dynasty (1271-1368). After destroyed in wartime, it was rebuilt together with the Drum Tower in the 18th year of Yong Le (1420), but soon, it was destroyed again, and rebuilt in the 10th year of Qian Long (1745). After two years, it was completed with a brick and stone structure to avoid fire disasters.

街衢巷陌

Streets and Lanes

正阳门大街
Zhengyangmen Street

[英国] 约翰·汤姆逊 [Britain] John Thomson

正阳门大街也称前门大街，位于北京中轴线，北起正阳门箭楼，南至天坛公园路口，与天桥南大街相连，是皇帝出城赴天坛、先农坛的御路，建外城后为外城主要南北街道。正阳门大街两侧为北京著名的商业区，京城百年老字号多聚于此。时至今日仍是北京最繁华热闹的大街之一。

照片中标志性建筑为位于正阳桥南的五牌楼，是正阳牌楼的俗称，因其造型形式为五间六柱五楼式而得名，正间额枋间镶"正阳桥"匾额。

正阳门城楼、箭楼、瓮城、正阳桥和五牌楼是一组布局合理、造型庄严、气势凝重的建筑群，是北京城的标志性建筑。

Also called Qianmen Street, Zhengyangmen Street is located on the capital's central axis. It links the watchtower of Zhengyangmen gate at the north end. Tiantan Park Street in the south, and the south Tianqiao Street in the middle. Used by emperors to leave for the Temple of Heaven or the Xiannong Temple, it became the main road from north to south in the Outer City after completion. Both sides of Zhengyangmen Street were a famous trading area, home of all Peking's time-honored brands. Today it is still one of Beijing's most bustling and lively streets.

The landmark architecture in the photo is the "Five Archway", the common name of the Zhengyang archway, located south of the Zhengyangqiao. The name stemmed from the five ways divided by six pillars. A wooden board was inlayed in the upper middle part, and inscribed with the three characters "Zheng Yang Qiao".

As one of Beijing's architectural landmarks, the gate tower, watchtower, barbican, Zhengyangqiao and the "Five Archway" of Zhengyangmen feature a reasonable layout, solemn design and imposing characters.

正阳门大街
Zhengyangmen Street

[德国] 阿尔方斯·冯·穆默 [Germany] Alfons von Mumm

街衢巷陌　　Streets and Lanes

崇文门内大街
Chongwenmen Inner Street

[德国] 海因茨·冯·佩克哈默 [Germany] Heinz v. Perckhammer

崇文门内大街位于北京内城南垣东侧，是一条南北走向的大街。此街地处交通要道，商业繁盛。清末民初，因其紧邻东交民巷使馆区，形成了主要为外国在华使馆及其侨民服务的商业区。

Running from north to south, Chongwenmen Inner Street was situated east to the southern wall of the Inner City. This important traffic route with prosperous business developed into an important business area offering services mainly to foreign embassies in China and to foreign residents in the late Qing Dynasty (1644-1911) and in the beginning of the Republic of China (1912-1949), because it was no far from the Dongjiaominxiang embassy district.

宣武门内大街
Xuanwumen Inner Street

[日本] 小川一真 [Japan] Kazuma Ogawa

宣武门内大街位于北京内城南垣西侧，是一条南北走向的大街。宣武门初称"顺承门"，后改称"宣武门"，此街名改为"宣武门街"。清朝，该街曾称"宣武门里街"、"宣武街"。1965年定名为"宣武门内大街"。

Running from north to south, Xuanwumen Inner Street was situated west to the southern wall of the Inner City. After Xuanwumen was used to replace "Shunchengmen", the street was also renamed as "Xuanwumen Street". Called "Xuanwumen Inner Street" and "Xuanwumen Street" in the Qing Dynasty (1644-1911), it finally received its current name in 1965.

地安门外大街
Di'anmen Outer Street

[法国] 阿尔贝·杜帖特 [France] Albert Dutertre

地安门外大街北起鼓楼，与鼓楼东西大街衔接，南至地安门，与地安门东、西大街及地安门内大街衔接。此街处于京城南北中轴线上，文物古迹遍布街道两旁，图中远处为鼓楼。

Spanning from the Drum Tower in the north to the Di'anmen in the south, Di'anmen Outer Street links the Drum Tower East and West Streets to the Di'anmen East, West and Inner Streets. Located on the north-south central axis, this street is famous for the cultural relics and historical sites on both sides. The building in the distance is the Drum Tower.

西直门内大街
Xizhimen Inner Street

[英国] 唐纳德·曼尼 [Britain] Donald Mennie

西直门内大街位于北京内城西垣北侧，是一条东西走向的大街。清代，这条大街是连接皇宫大内与西郊三山五园的主要通道。

Running from west to east, Xizhimen Inner Street was located north to the western wall of the Inner City. In the Qing Dynasty (1644-1911), it was the main street to link the Imperial Palace with the hills and gardens in the western outskirts.

朝阳门内大街
Chaoyangmen Inner Street

[日本] 小川一真 [Japan] Kazuma Ogawa

朝阳门，元代称齐化门，明代更名为朝阳门，位于内城东垣南侧。照片为 20 世纪初的朝阳门内大街。

Named as Qihuamen in the Yuan Dynasty (1271-1368), Chaoyangmen got its current name in the Ming Dynasty (1368-1644) and was located south to the eastern wall of the Inner City. The photo shows the Chaoyangmen Inner Street in the 1900s.

德胜门外的街道
Street Outside Deshengmen

[日本] 小川一真 [Japan] Kazuma Ogawa

德胜门，元代称健德门，明代更名为德胜门，位于内城北垣西侧。照片为在德胜门上看到的城外街道。

Named as Jiandemen in the Yuan Dynasty (1271-1368), Deshengmen got its current name in the Ming Dynasty (1368-1644), and was located west to the northern wall of the Inner City. The photo shows the street out of the gate.

街衢巷陌　　Streets and Lanes

安定门内大街
Andingmen Inner Street

[英国]唐纳德·曼尼 [Britain] Donald Mennie

安定门内大街位于北京内城北垣东侧，是一条南北走向的大街。宽阔笔直的大街被左右两条砖砌的排水沟划分为三部分，道路中间供行人行走和轿车行驶，外侧为便道，供大车和骆驼队行驶。道路两边店铺林立。

Running from north to south, the Andingmen Inner Street was located east to the northern wall of the Inner City. Among the three lanes divided by two brick-made drainage gutters in this broad and straight street, the middle lane was for pedestrians and cars, and the outer lanes were for cart and camel caravans. On both sides of the street were shops in great numbers.

安定门外大街
Andingmen Outer Street

[日本] 小川一真 [Japan] Kazuma Ogawa

安定门外大街位于北京内城北侧。明清时此街是一条通向北方的大道。明清皇帝去地坛祭祀时必走此街，故又称为御路。

As a street stretching northward, the Andingmen Outer Street was located at the north of the Inner City. It was commonly referred to as the Imperial Road because emperors offering sacrifices in the Temple of Earth in the Ming and Qing Dynasties (1368-1644,1644-1911) had to pass through this street.

东长安街
East Chang'an Avenue

长安街以天安门为界，往东为东长安街，往西为西长安街。其名取自盛唐时代的都城——长安（今陕西西安），意为长治久安。

Tian'anmen divided the Chang'an Avenue into two parts, the West Chang'an Avenue and the East Chang'an Avenue. It is named after the great capital city, Chang'an (today Xi'an) of the Tang Dynasty (618-907), meaning lasting peace and stability.

[法国] 阿尔贝·杜帖特 [France] Albert Dutertre

西长安街
West Chang'an Avenue

佚名 Unknown Photographer

街衢巷陌　　Streets and Lanes

鼓楼东大街
Drum Tower East Street

[英国] 唐纳德·曼尼 [Britain] Donald Mennie

鼓楼东大街西起鼓楼，东至交道口大街，因位于鼓楼东侧而得名。自元大都时，鼓楼地区即被规划为商业区，并成为元、明、清三朝的繁华闹市。站在鼓楼上俯瞰鼓楼东大街，宽阔笔直的大街通向远方的东直门。

Linking the Drum Tower in the west and the Jiaodaokou Street in the east, Drum Tower East Street got its name for its location east to the Drum Tower. After being planned as a business area in the Yuan Dynasty (1271-1368), the Drum Tower area became a bustling shopping centre not only in that dynasty but also the following two eras. The wide and straight street extended to Dongzhimen in the distance.

户部街
Hubu Street

[德国] 海因茨·冯·佩克哈默 [Germany] Heinz v. Perckhammer

户部街位于棋盘街东面之北，街东为宗人府、吏部、户部、礼部等。民国十七年（1928）改名为公安街。照片中的现代楼房建筑为民国四年（1915）利用礼部旧址改建的邮政总局。照片中左边为环有白石栏杆的"天街"（俗称"棋盘街"）。

Located north to the east section of Qipan Street, Hubu Street was home to government agencies of China, the Imperial Clan Court, the Ministry of Official Personnel Affairs, the Ministry of Revenue and the Ministry of Rites, etc. It was renamed Gong'an Street in the Republic of China's 17th year (1928). The modern building in the picture was the General Post Office, reconstructed on the site of the Ministry of Rites in the Republic of China's fourth year (1915). On the left side was Tianjie, enclosed by white stone fences, commonly referred to as Qipan Street.

王府井大街
Wangfujing Street

[日本] 开发忍 [Japan] Shinobu Kaihatsu

王府井大街南起东长安街，北至东四西大街西口。辽、金时代，王府井原是一个不出名的小村落，元代以后，人烟逐渐稠密，称为丁字街。明代时，此处修建了十座王府，遂称十王府街，清代废十王，改称为王府街或王府大街。清末，随着东交民巷使馆界的开辟，王府井大街南段商业发达。1903年，东安市场开业，此后王府井也愈加繁荣。

Stretching from the East Chang'an Avenue in the south and the west end of the Dongsi West Street in the north, Wangfujing Street was a non-famous village road in the Liao and Jin Dynasties (907-1125, 1115-1234). It was named Dingzi Street in the Yuan Dynasty (1271-1368) when more households moved here. It was called Shiwangfu Street in the Ming Dynasty (1368-1644) when ten royal prince residences (wangfu) were built here. It was renamed as Wangfu Street or Wangfu Avenue in the Qing Dynasty(1644-1911), when the royal court discarded ten-prince system. The southern section of it prospered and became westernized during the late Qing Dynasty, when the embassy district at Dongjiaominxiang was built and commerce developed. It became more prosperous after Dong'an Market was opened here in 1903.

西单大街
Xidan Street

[日本] 开发忍 [Japan] Shinobu Kaihatsu

西单大街商业繁荣，最早可追溯到明代。

The history of the bustling Xidan Street could be traced back to the Ming Dynasty (1368-1644).

街衢巷陌　　Streets and Lanes

东单大街
Dongdan Street

[日本] 儿岛鹭麿 [Japan] Sagimaro Kojima

东单北大街在明清时就已形成，清光绪时称就日坊北大街，因街南端东单牌楼而得名。附近有东单二条、东单三条胡同。此照为清朝末年的东单大街。

Starting to develop since the Ming and Qing Dynasties, Dongdan North Street was called Jiurifang North Street during the reign of Emperor Guangxu (1875-1908) in the late Qing Dynasty (1644-1911). Named after Dongdan Archway at its south end, it links lanes like Dongdan Ertiao and Dongdan Santiao. The photo shows Dongdan Street in the late Qing Dynasty.

京 华 旧 影
Old Photos of Beijing

大高玄殿牌坊
Dagaoxuandian Archways

[英国] 约翰·汤姆逊 [Britain] John Thomson

大高玄殿又称大高殿，是明清两代皇家道观，建于明嘉靖二十一年（1542），位于景山前街，该殿坐北朝南，大高殿门外有东、西、南三座牌坊和习礼亭两座，牌楼均为四柱九楼，习礼亭为九梁十八柱，造型奇巧，为最高等级的道教建筑。图中为西牌坊，匾额正面镌"弘佑天民"，背面镌"太极仙林"，1960年原牌楼移至中共中央党校，现在院内掠燕湖的北岸。

Also called Dagaodian, Dagaoxuandian was a royal Taoist temple in the Ming and Qing Dynasties (1368-1644, 1644-1911). Built in the 21st of Jia Jing (1542) at Jingshan Front Street, this south-facing hall was joined by three archways at the east, west and south side of its gate and two pavilions for "exercising the rites". The nine-eave archways were supported by four pillars each and the pavilions were composed of nine beams and eighteen pillars. The ingenious and exquisite architecture was regarded as the highest grade Taoist building in China at the time. The photo shows the west archway, whose wooden board reading "Hongyou Tianmin (grand blessings to the celestial nation)" on its front side and "Taiji Xianlin(the wonderful views of the Great Ultimate)" on its back. The archway was relocated to the north bank of Lake Lueyanhu inside the Party School of the Central Committee of C.P.C, in 1960.

街衢巷陌　　Streets and Lanes

东单牌楼和西单牌楼
Dongdan Archway and Xidan Archway

京 华 旧 影
Old Photos of Beijing

佚名 Unknown Photographer

东单牌楼和西单牌楼分别位于东西长安街尽头，各一座，故称"单牌楼"，均为三间四柱三楼冲天式。东单牌楼匾额上刻有"就日"二字，西单牌楼匾额上刻有"瞻云"二字，1916年袁世凯分别改为"景星"和"庆云"。两牌楼均已不存。

Dongdan and Xidan archways, also called Single Archway which are wooden structures of four towering pillars, were located at the east and west ends of Chang'an Avenue respectively. They feature plaques inscribed with the words "Jiuri" and "Zhanyun" respectively, which were changed into "Jingxing" and "Qingyun" by Yuan Shikai in 1916. Neither exists at present day.

街衢巷陌　　Streets and Lanes

东四牌楼
Dongsi Archways

[美国] 西德尼·D·甘博 [America] Sidney D. Gamble

西四牌楼
Xisi Archways

[日本] 山本赞七郎 [Japan] Sanshichiro Yamamoto

东四牌楼和西四牌楼均修建于明朝,为三间四柱三楼冲天式木牌楼。因在紫禁城北门神武门向东、西各三里的十字路口,分别修建了四座牌楼,故称"东四牌楼"和"西四牌楼",均于1954年被拆除。

Erected in the Ming Dynasty(1368-1644), both Dongsi and Xisi archways feature wooden structures, supported by four towering pillars. They were so named because they were the archways built at the road crossings east and west from Shenwumen, the north gate of the Forbidden City. The crossings were three li (1.5 kilometers) away from each others. They were all demolished in 1954.

东交民巷西口牌楼
Archway at the West End of Dongjiaominxiang Street

[法国] 阿尔贝·杜帖特 [France] Albert Dutertre

东交民巷西口牌楼为三开间式仿木牌楼，名"敷文"。此牌楼是 1915 年袁世凯为筹备登基所建。于 1954 年拆除。

With four pillars made of wood-like material, the archway at the west end of Dongjiaominxiang Street was named as "Fuwen". Built in 1915 by Yuan Shikai in preparation for ascending the throne, it was removed in 1954.

北京外城街景
Street Scenery at Beijing's Outer City

[瑞典] 奥斯伍尔德·喜仁龙 [Sweden] Osvald Siren

北京外城是明嘉靖三十二年（1553）修建，相对于内城而被称为外城。在清朝时期北京外城的商业、戏楼、酒馆，随着各行各业人才的到来而发展繁荣起来。

Constructed in the 32nd year of Jia Jing (1553), the Outer City of Beijing got its name because it was outside the Inner City. In the Qing Dynasty (1644-1911), shops, opera houses and taverns flourished here with the arrival of people of all professions and skills.

御河
Yuhe

[德国] 阿尔方斯·冯·穆默 [Germany] Alfons von Mumm

御河（玉河），是元时的通惠河故道，明清时称为玉河。以河道为界西岸称西河沿，东岸称东河沿。民国时东河沿称正义路，西河沿称兴国路。御河改为暗沟后，1965年统称正义路。此照为从南向北拍摄。

Named as the Jade River in the Ming and Qing Dynasties (1368-1644, 1644-1911), Yuhe was a section of the watercourse of the Tonghuihe . The west and east banks were called Xiheyan and Dongheyan respectively and renamed as Xingguo Road and Zhengyi Road during the Republic of China (1912-1949). Both sides were called Zhengyi Road after the river was covered in 1965. This picture was taken in the south.

高粱桥
Gaoliang Bridge

佚名 Unknown Photographer

高粱桥位于北京西直门外，始建于元代，是一座青白石单孔拱桥。

Built in Yuan Dynasty (1271-1368) outside of Xizhimen, the Gaoliang Bridge was a single arched bridge made of greenish white marble.

大通桥
Datong Bridge

佚名 Unknown Photographer

大通桥位于东便门外，原为一座石桥，为了方便行人进出城所建。该桥南北走向，为三孔联拱石桥，中孔极大，两侧孔较小，三个券洞上方雕有兽头。因位置较特殊，桥西为内城的护城河，桥东为通惠河，故命名"大通桥"。

Located outside of Dongbianmen, Datong Bridge was originally built for the convenience of pedestrians. Linking the north and south banks, it was a stone bridge featuring a giant opening in the middle and two smaller openings on both sides. All the openings were decorated with carved animal heads above them. Because the bridge sat in conjunction of the city moat in the west and the Tonghuihe in the east, it was called Datong Bridge.

京 华 旧 影
Old Photos of Beijing

街头洒水养路
Sprinkling Water to Maintain the Streets

老北京的道路多为土路或石渣路，为了养护路面，有专人进行洒水养路。

To maintain the streets which were mostly unpaved or made of crushed stones, workers were hired to sprinkle water on them.

［美国］西德尼·D·甘博 [America] Sidney D. Gamble

［日本］岩田秀则 [Japan] Hidenori Iwata

街衢巷陌　　Streets and Lanes

风俗节令

Customs and Festivals

隆福寺庙会
Longfu Temple Fair

佚名 Unknown Photographer

隆福寺位于东四十字路口的西北角，始建于明景泰三年（1452），清雍正九年（1731）重修，是朝廷的香火院之一。隆福寺庙会曾是京城的四大庙会之一。清代农历每月逢一、二、九、十开庙，民国时改用阳历一、二、九、十开庙。每逢庙会，人流如潮，可以买到各种土特产品，看到民间戏曲，品尝各式各样的北京小吃。庙会的摊位通常从一进山门就开始，前殿多是卖古玩、珠宝的摊商，二院以后则是卖日用百货、衣服鞋帽、首饰、布匹、儿童玩具的，著名的有王麻子的刀剪、金象张的梳头篦子、钢刀刘的茶果刀等。照片为隆福寺后院（塔院）的小吃和游艺的摊位，中间夹杂着相面、算卦、卖药的。

Located at the northwestern corner of the Dongsi crossroads, Longfu Temple was built in the third year of Jing Tai (1452) and reconstructed in the 9th year of Yong Zheng(1731). It was not only one of the Royal temples, but was also famous for its fair, one of the four largest in Beijing. In the Qing Dynasty (1644-1911), it was celebrated at the first, second, ninth and tenth day of each lunar month. In the period of the Republic of China (1912-1949), it was celebrated on the same days of the solar months. At the temple fairs, crowds of people came in to buy native products, to see folk operas and to taste Beijing Snacks. Stalls linked the temple gate and the halls. In the front hall, antiques and jewelry were sold; in the second yard, articles of daily use, clothes, shoes, headgears, headdresses, fabric and toys for children were available. Among them, Wangmazi's knives and scissors, Jinxiangzhang's combs, and Gangdaoliu's fruit knives were very popular. The photo shows the stalls for snacks and entertainment the back yard (tower yard) of the Longfu Temple, that are mixed up with stalls for forture telling and medicine selling.

风俗节令　　Customs and Festivals

隆福寺庙会
Longfu Temple Fair

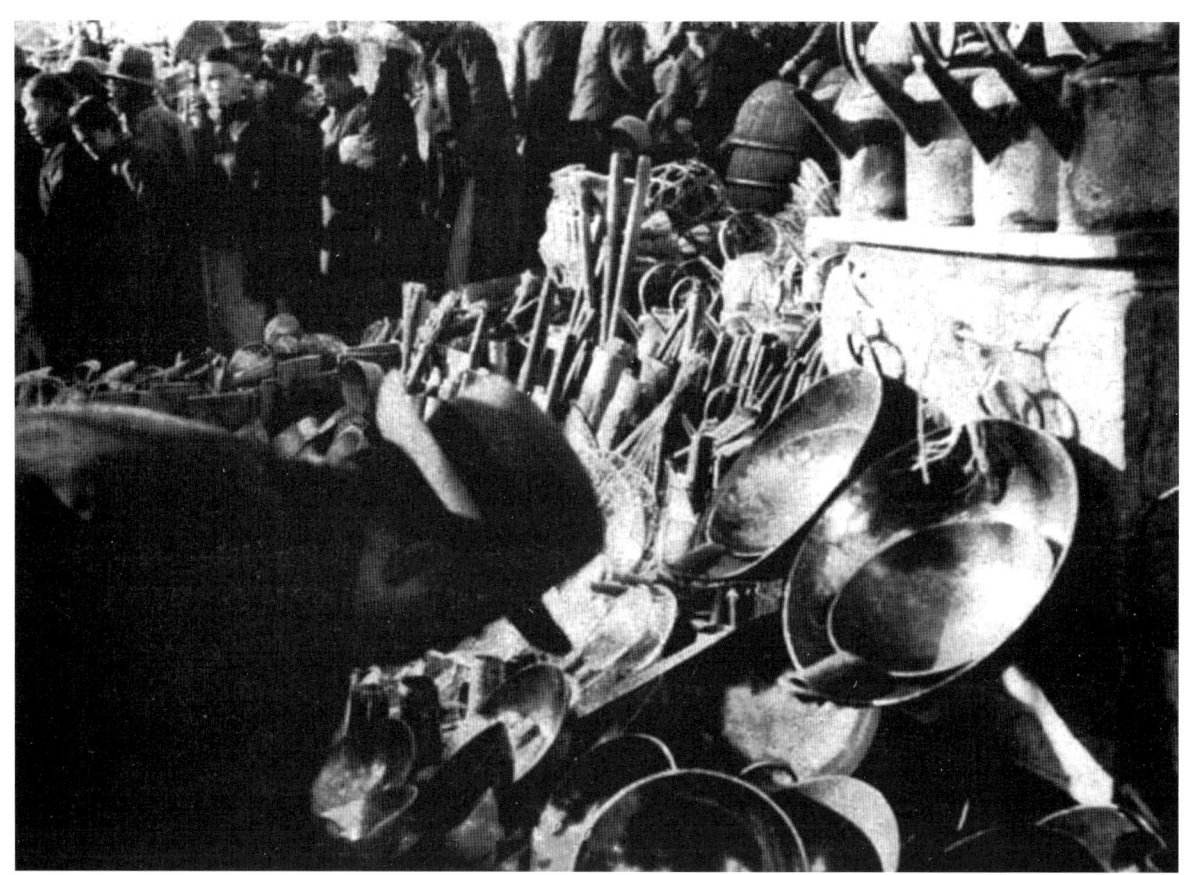

佚名 Unknown Photographer

隆福寺庙会的蜡管留声机
The Wax Cylinder Phonograph at Longfu Temple Fair

蜡管留声机播放的是唱片，唱片的前身是蜡筒录音。在留声机上放送时需接上几根橡皮管子，听者将管子塞在耳朵上才能听到。当时北京的东安市场、隆福寺，都有这样的留声机摊子，花上几文钱，就可以听上一段，有点像听觉上的拉洋片。

Disc records were played on the wax cylinder phonograph, The former form of the recording disc was wax cylinder records. When music was played by a phonograph, a listener had to plug in several plastic tubes and put the other side of the tubes into their ears. At that time, there were many such phonograph stalls in Dong'an Market and Longfu Temple in Beijing. With a little money, people could listen to a piece of the records, which was like hearing a peepshow.

佚名 Unknown Photographer

蟠桃宫庙会
Temple fair at the Peach Palace

蟠桃宫，道教宫观，位于东便门内护城河南岸。照片为蟠桃宫前殿内景，供奉着西王母娘娘，还筑有一座鳌山，山上有众仙腾云前来为王母娘娘祝寿的塑像。

相传农历三月初三是王母娘娘的寿诞，会举行蟠桃盛会，故每年农历三月初一至初三，蟠桃宫举办庙会。庙会期间有大鼓、单弦、相声、变戏法等艺人在庙外献艺；高跷、十不闲、舞狮、旱船也来此朝拜。做生意的小商贩的摊位更是连绵数里。

The Peach Palace was a Taoist temple, located on the south bank of the city moat at the downtown side of Dongbianmen. The photo shows the interior of the front hall, dedicated to the Queen Mother of the West. A sculpture mountain was also built, showing all the immortals stepping forward on the clouds to celebrate her birthday.

According to legend, at the Queen Mother's birthday on March 3rd of the lunar calendar, a grand party was to be held at the Peach Palace. Therefore, The Peach Palace held a temple fair from March 1st to 3rd of the lunar calendar each year, during which artistic performances like beating a big drum, playing the one-string fiddle, comic dialogues and conjuring tricks were staged outside the temple. Stilt dancers, Shibuxian Singers, lion dancers and running ship dancers also joined the celebration. Small vendors set up numerous stalls covering several miles.

佚名 Unknown Photographer

旧时北京求子"拴娃娃"者众多，人们手腕缠红绳，到蟠桃宫东配殿献上香资后拴住一个殿前摆放的泥娃娃带回家，与子结缘。照片为蟠桃宫兴盛的香火，女人们正在燃香求娘娘保佑，平安吉顺，祈求子嗣。

In the old days, many people in Beijing went to the east side hall of the Pantao Temple praying for pregnancy. They tied red strings on the clay dolls in front of the hall, and took them home after burning incense, in order to pray for a baby. The photo shows incense at the temple, by which women prayed to the Queen Mother of the West for blessings, protection, luck, and babies.

佚名 Unknown Photographer

风俗节令　　Customs and Festivals

白塔寺庙会
White Pagoda Temple Fair

佚名 Unknown Photographer

白塔寺庙会形成于清末民初。因当时寺内香火不旺，僧人出租部分寺庙庙产，招来不同行业的商贩开店，这里逐渐成为京城的闹市。开始庙会为旧历每月逢五、六开市。后改为逢三、四、五、六开市。

White Pagoda Temple Fair started in the late Qing Dynasty (1644-1911) and the beginning of the Republic of China (1912-1949). Due to the lack of donations by worshippers, monks of the temple leased out some properties to attract merchants to do business in the temple, which turned this place into a bustling market. Initially held only on the fifth and sixth day of each lunar month, the fair was also open on the third and fourth day of lunar months in the later days.

佚名 Unknown Photographer

佚名 Unknown Photographer

小贩们用棉线将山里红穿成串，斜背肩上，挎于肘上，在庙会间游走叫卖。

Venders selling hawthorn fruit which they linked by cotton string and carried over their shoulders or arms, while pacing around the temple fair.

风 俗 节 令　　　Customs and Festivals

妙峰山庙会
Miaofengshan Temple Fair

佚名 Unknown Photographer

妙峰山位于门头沟区妙峰山镇涧沟村，是一座汇集了佛教、道教、民间信仰的名山。妙峰山庙会始于明朝崇祯年间，农历四月初一至十五和七月二十五至八月初一举办春香庙会和秋香庙会各一次，以春香庙会为最盛。由于妙峰山供奉着碧霞元君、眼光娘娘、释迦牟尼、观音等神灵，各路香客到此均有神可拜、有佛可依，所以妙峰山庙会成了京城及邻近各省香火极盛之所。据说妙峰山的福祉照远不照近，故每年阳春四月除北京、天津、保定等地的香客外，远自吉林、川贵、湖广，甚至日本、东南亚等地也有人来烧香还愿。

Located in Jian'gou Village of Miaofengshan Township, in Mentougou District. Miaofengshan is a famous mountain that brings together Buddhism, Taoism and folk beliefs. Since the reign of Chong Zhen Emperor (1628-1644) of the Ming Dynasty, Miaofengshan Temple Fair was held from April 1st to 15th and from July 25th to August 1st of the lunar calendar, of which the first event is always the most popular. Different gods were worshipped in Miaofengshan, like Bixia Yuanjun, Yan'guang Niangniang, Shakyamuni and Guanyin. Everyone had a deity to pray to, therefore, the temple Fair became the most attractive place for worshippers from Beijing and the outer provinces. It is said that the guests from afar were especially blessed by the gods in Miaofengshan. Thus a lot of pilgrims came here every April of the lunar calendar, not only from Beijing, Tianjin or Baoding, but also from distant provinces, such as Jilin, Sichuan, Guizhou, Hubei, Hunan, Guangdong or Guangxi, even from Japan and Southeast Asia.

佚名 Unknown Photographer

到妙峰山进香的香客除独行、全家、朋友结伴外，还有许多人专门为进香而结成团体，即香会。香会少则二三人，多则有成千上万人。香会由德高望重、有组织能力的老年人任会长。通常前面有铜锣开道，后面有手执锤铜的壮士，依次有灵官旗、小车会、秧歌会、大鼓会等，此外还有若干面神幡、村名幡穿插在队伍当中。"娘娘神驾"走在队伍之中，后面跟着"号佛会"，神旗殿后。民间花会的表演也成为妙峰山庙会的重头戏。

The pilgrims came to Miaofengshan alone, with their families, friends, or in groups called pilgrim associations. With members ranging from several to tens of thousands, the associations were headed by the elderly with noble character, high prestige and organization ability. Usually gong players were in front of the pilgrim procession, followed by warriors playing hammers and maces, a banner of the deity, carriages, folk dance groups, and then drum ensembles, etc. Some long narrow flags for the gods or with village names could also be found. The "Palanquin of the Holy Lady" was carried in the middle of the procession, followed by "Praising Buddha" performers and holy flags. Folk performances were also an important part of the show during the temple fair of Miaofengshan.

风 俗 节 令　　　Customs and Festivals

腊八
Laba Festival

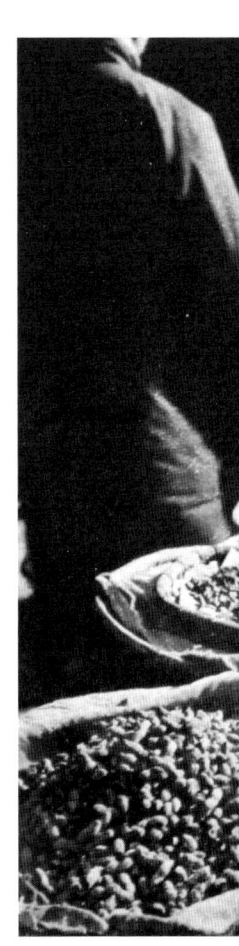

农历十二月初八为腊八节，俗称"腊八"，原意是祭祀祖先和神灵，祈求丰收、吉祥和避邪。喝腊八粥的习俗最早始于宋代，到了清朝，喝腊八粥的风俗更是盛行。自雍正皇帝起，朝廷在这天都有赐粥风俗。在雍和宫用数口大锅熬粥，由喇嘛诵经，并派大臣前往拈香上祭。各道院以舍粥为善，民间百姓以粥敬神，亲朋好友互送腊八粥，以增加情感。

左边照片为1941年京城内粥铺给贫民施腊八粥的场景。右边照片为腊八之前售卖腊八粥所用桂圆、莲子、果仁等各类食材的摊位。

The December 8th of the lunar calendar is the Laba festival, also called "Laba", This is a time to offer sacrifices to ancestors and gods, pray for good harvest and luck, and to exorcise evils. The custom of having porridge on that day began in the Song Dynasty (960-1279) and became more popular in the Qing Dynasty (1644-1911). Started by Emperor Yong Zheng, the court started a practice of handing out porridge to the people, which continued year by year. In Yonghegong lama Temple, porridge cooked in big pots was given out after Lamas chanted the sutras and a minister burned incense and offered sacrifices. Temples offered porridge to people for free, the common people worshipped the gods with porridge, friends and relatives also presented it to each other to enhance their bonds.

The photo on the left shows a porridge kitchen, where the porridge was given to the poor in Beijing in 1941. The photo on the right shows a market stall, which sold all kind of ingredients for the porridge, like longans, lotus seeds, nuts and pips before the Laba Festival.

佚名 Unknown Photographer

风 俗 节 令　　　Customs and Festivals

采办年货
Holiday Shopping

佚名 Unknown Photographer

春节是中国人最大的节日。旧京向有"忙年"一说，一到腊月，即开始筹备过年的诸般事宜，其中最主要的就是置办年货。除服装、食品、日用品之外，还要购买祭祀用品、烟花爆竹、年画、春联及为孩子和大人买的玩具、灯笼等。一进腊月，街市中人头攒动，拥挤不堪。

The Spring Festival (Chinese New Year) is the most important holiday for the Chinese people. There was a saying of "Mang Nian" (lots of preparations lasting for a week before the Chinese New Year) in old Beijing. In the beginning of "La Yue" (the twelfth lunar month of a year), families started to prepare everything for the New Year. Among all the preparations, "Ban Nian Huo" (purchases for the Spring Festival) is quite a big deal. Apart from clothes, cuisine and other daily necessities, people also needed to buy the paraphernalia for worshipping, firecrackers, "Nian Hua" (New Year pictures), "Chun Lian" (New Year couplets), and other items for children and adults, such as, lanterns, toys, etc. When the twelfth lunar month approaches, streets would be crowded because of the many people and vendors.

除夕踩岁
Crushing Stalks on New Year's Eve

佚名 Unknown Photographer

除夕，又称大年夜。守岁、压岁和踩岁是除夕极富特色的三种祈福形式。踩岁风俗是在除夕之日将芝麻秸铺到院内或甬路上，家人出入，踩踏其上，噼啪作响。天黑时，全家老少将其全部踩碎，取辞旧岁迎新岁、岁岁平安之意。"岁"与"祟"谐音，所以也有踩去一年晦气之意。有的人家还会在芝麻秸下撒些铜钱，小孩在芝麻秸踩碎后，会惊喜地捡到铜钱，预示来年吉祥。照片为年轻女子在除夕夜踩岁。

On New Year's Eve, people pray for luck with three special customs: being awake all night, presenting gift-money and crushing stalks. Sesame stalks were strewed in the yard or on the sidewalks, to create crackling noise when the people stepped on them. In the night, all the family members crushed all the stalks in order to welcome the New Year and to pray for safety. "Year" and "evils" are homophonic in Chinese, so crushing stalks, also called "caisui"(crushing years) means destroying the bad luck of the last year. Sometimes, some copper coins would be hidden under the stalks and picked up by kids, indicating an auspicious new year. The photo shows a Chinese girl crushing stalks on New Year's Eve.

除夕包饺子
Making Dumplings on New Year's Eve

佚名 Unknown Photographer

北京人的年夜饭习惯吃饺子。吃饺子的习俗是从汉朝传下来的，取新旧交替"更岁交子"的意思。饺子因为形状像银元宝，一盆盆端上桌又象征着"新年大发财，元宝滚进来"之意。过年时全家人要一起包饺子，体现一家人的团结和睦。有的饺子还会放一些洗净的硬币和枣，讨个吉利。照片为1943年前后除夕夜全家包饺子的场景。

People in Beijing eat dumplings on New Year's Eve. Originating from the Han Dynasty (202BC-220AD), this custom started because "Jiaozi (dumpling)" and "year changes" are homophonic in Chinese. Moreover, the shape of the dumpling is similar to sycees (traditional silver ingot currency), dumplings served in bowls symbolized the wish of earning more money in the New Year. Family members sitting together making dumplings manifested family unity and harmony. Cleaned coins or dates sometimes would be put inside dumplings as lucky charms. The photo shows the whole family making dumplings on New Year's Eve around 1943.

拜祭祖先
Ancestral Worship

[德国] 赫达·莫里逊 [Germany] Hedda Morrison

除夕、清明、中元、重阳是中国传统祭祖的四大节日，其中，除夕之夜祭祀祖先是一项重要的礼俗。照片为民国时期某个富裕家庭里男孩在春节时叩拜祖先。

New Year's Eve, Tomb-Sweeping Day, Hungry Ghost Festival, and Double Ninth Festival are the four important traditional festivals for the Chinese to worship their ancestors. Among them, the worship on New Year's Eve is a very important custom. The photo shows a boy in a wealthy family kowtowing before his ancestors during the Republic of China period (1912-1949).

新年祭祖
Ancestral Worship on New Year's Eve

佚名 Unknown Photographer

老北京人家都供有佛龛或神像，各大年节通常会在家中将祖先牌位依次摆在正厅，陈列供品，然后祭拜者按长幼顺序上香跪拜。除夕夜要摆上九堂大供，家境不好的也要摆三堂或五堂供品。除夕夜和元旦供素煮饽饽，每日早晚焚香叩头，献供新茶。照片为1943年前后北京家庭新年祭祖的供桌。

People whose families have settled in Beijing for generations put the tablets of their ancestors in sequence in niches or in front of Buddha statues in their main hall for every New Year's Eve and other important festivals. The descendants would kowtow and burn incense in sequence according to their seniority in the family. On New Year's Eve, many offerings would be made, and even poor families would offer something to their ancestors. Besides offering cooked pastries without meat on New Year's Eve and the following days, people in Beijing also worshipped every morning and evening by burning incense, kowtowing, and presenting a new cup of tea. The photo shows the worship table of a Beijing family around 1943.

京 华 旧 影
Old Photos of Beijing

拜年
Paying a Ceremonial Visit on the New Year

[德国] 海因茨·冯·佩克哈默 [Germany] Heinz v. Perckhammer

拜年是中国民间的传统习俗，是人们辞旧迎新的一种方式。农历正月初一为一年之初，除了自家庆贺外，人们都出门走亲访友，相互拜年，恭祝来年大吉大利。照片为平辈间的礼节性拜年，彼此抱拳拱手一揖，说些祝福的吉利话。

Paying a ceremonial visit is a Chinese folk custom at the end of the previous year and beginning of a new one. On January 1st of the lunar calendar, people celebrate not just at home, but also visit relatives and friends to wish them good luck. The photo shows a ceremonial visit paid on New Year by two men of the same generation, who bowed to each other with hands folded in front while saying auspicious words.

风 俗 节 令　　Customs and Festivals

元宵摊位
Market Stalls Selling Yuanxiao Dumplings

佚名 Unknown Photographer

农历正月十五是元宵节,又称"上元节"。这天全家会团聚吃元宵、赏花灯、猜灯谜。正月十五吃元宵意在祝愿全家团圆,诸事圆满。自正月初六开始,各大饽饽铺即开始售卖元宵,至十三日上灯时,大饽饽铺便在棚里支出案子,摆出大笸箩,当众摇制元宵。照片为1940年前后京城售卖元宵的摊位前繁忙的景象。

On the night of the Lantern Festival or Shangyuan Festival, on January 15th of the lunar calendar, members of a family gathers together, eat Yuanxiao (sweet dumplings made of glutinous rice flour), appreciate colorful lanterns, and play with riddles written on lanterns. Eating Yuanxiao on that day represents the wish of a family for unity and success. Starting from January 6th of the lunar calendar, pastry shops begin to sell Yuanxiao. On January 13th when lanterns began to be displayed, pastry shops begin to show the process of making Yuanxiao on the tables outside and show them in big baskets. The photo shows a busy Yuanxiao-making stalls around 1940.

元宵观灯
Appreciating Lanterns at the Lantern Festival

元宵节赏灯是北京的一大盛事。家家户户都悬挂五色彩灯，彩灯上画有各种图案，花灯焰火照耀通宵，十分繁华热闹。照片为1940年前后北京城元宵节观灯的游行队伍。

Appreciating lanterns during the Lantern Festival is an important activity in Beijing. Every family hangs colorful lanterns painted with all sorts of patterns, shining at night over the bustling crowd. The photo shows a lantern procession during the Lantern Festival in Beijing around 1940.

佚名 Unknown Photographer

佚名 Unknown Photographer

风俗节令　Customs and Festivals

烧火判
Burning the Judge

佚名 Unknown Photographer

烧火判是老北京灯节上特有的一项民俗活动。"判"指的是阴间掌管生死簿的判官。京城烧火判主要有两处，即琉璃厂海王村公园外的吕祖祠和地安门外西侧皇城根路北的宛平县城隍庙。正月十三到十七，城隍庙正院安放一尊三四米高的泥塑空心判官，头戴双翅乌纱帽，手持"黑无常"勾魂牌，腹中是用砖砌成的、能装 200 斤煤的大炉灶。生火后判官烧得浑身通红，耳口鼻眼、肚脐双乳都能喷出火来，煞是威武。传说，凡捐煤烧火判的买卖家，来年必定生意红火。照片为元宵节在宛平县城隍庙出现的烧火判。

Burning the Judge was a unique custom during the Lantern Festival in Beijing. The "Judge" here refers to the judge in the underworld who registers the living and the dead. It was burned usually at two places in Beijing, one at the Lv Zu Temple outside Haiwangcun Park at Liulichang, and the other at the Wanping Town God Temple, north of Huang chenggen Street, in the west outside Di'anmen. From January 13th to the 17th of the lunar calendar, a three-or-four-meters-high clay statue of the underworld judge would set in the main yard of the Town God Temple, with an official cap of black gauze on his head and a soul-capturing tablet in his hand. Inside his body was a brick stove which could hold 100kg of coals. The body with the stove burning inside was glowing red, with fire emitting from his ears, mouth, nose, eyes, navel and nipples. It is said that such a powerful burning judge would bless all the merchants donating coals with booming business in the following year. The photo shows the judge at Wanping Town God Temple.

端午节艾叶辟邪
Mugwort Leaves Counteracting Evil Spirits at the Dragon Boat Festival

佚名 Unknown Photographer

农历五月初五的端午节是夏季驱除瘟疫的节日，家家要在街门外斜插菖蒲、艾叶，号称"蒲剑"、"艾虎"。此时气候湿热，多生病毒瘟疫，古人认为这是一种"邪祟"。为躲避邪祟，攘除不祥，民间有"端午到，插艾蒿"的风俗。菖蒲通常被认为是天中五瑞之首，象征驱除不祥的宝剑，插在门口可以辟邪。艾草则代表百福，插在门口可保身体健康。照片为端午节宅门上辟邪的艾叶，门楣上高悬朱墨绘的钟馗像。

The Dragon Boat Festival on May 5th of the lunar calendar is an occasion for driving away epidemic diseases in the summer. For that purpose, every family placed calami or mugwort leaves at its front gate, calling it "calami sword" or "mugwort tiger", which was used to counter evil spirits that was believed to be the cause of summer epidemics when it was damp and hot. Calami was believed to be the strongest sword to defeat evil forces while mugwort leaves could ensure healthiness and good luck of family members. The photo shows mugwort leaves hanging above a front gate, which was decorated by a red-inked portrait of Zhong Kui, a vanquisher of evil beings.

中元节放荷灯
Lighting Lotus Lamps at the Ghost Festival

佚名 Unknown Photographer

农历七月十五日为中元节，传说这一日地府放出全部鬼魂，民间普遍进行祭祀鬼魂的活动。这一节日也成为中国民间最大的祭祀节日之一。放荷灯是中元节夜晚超度亡灵的重要民俗活动。人们用彩纸做成朵朵莲花，下面用西瓜或南瓜作底托，中间插上点燃的蜡烛，放在水面，无数的荷灯在水中缓缓移动，闪闪烁烁，灿若繁星，蔚为奇观。照片为中元节夜晚北海公园湖面上放荷灯。

According to folk legend, at the Zhongyuan Festival (Ghost Festival), on July 15th of the lunar calendar, all ghosts would come out of the nether world. In this festival of sacrifices, which is widely celebrated in China, people have a custom of offering sacrifices to ghosts, by lighting lotus lamps in the evening of that day. It is said that the lamps which are made of colorful paper and put inside melons or pumpkins will show souls the way out of purgatory. With a candle light in each, the lamps are put on the water. Numerous sparkling lamps, shining like stars, form an amazing spectacle. The photo shows lotus lamps during Zhongyuan Festival in Beihai Park.

风俗节令　　Customs and Festivals

北海公园的盂兰法会
Ullambana at Beihai Park

农历七月十五日，旧时京城内较大的佛教寺庙在这一天都举办盂兰法会。供奉佛祖和僧人，济度六道苦难，以及报谢父母养育慈爱之恩。民国以后，北海公园、中山公园等各大公园每年有官方举办的"追悼阵亡将士法会"。图为摆在北海琉璃牌坊后边的法船，当晚用人抬着，僧道随后，送至小西天空旷处焚烧。

Some large Buddhist temples in Beijing held Ullambana ceremonies on July 15th of the lunar calendar, during which sacrifices were offered to the Buddha and the monks for the salvation of all beings and the appreciation of parents' love. Since the Republic of China period, the "memorial ceremony for martyrs" was officially held every year at big parks like Beihai Park, Zhongshan Park or other parks. The photo shows a paper boat which was put behind the glazed archway of Beihai Park before being moved (followed by monks) to Xiaoxitian where it would be burnt for blessings.

佚名 Unknown Photographer

风俗节令　　Customs and Festivals

中元节盂兰法会
Ullambana at the Ghost Festival

佚名 Unknown Photographer

农历七月十五道教宫观要举办"祈福吉祥道场",祈祷风调雨顺、国泰民安。晚间施放焰火,超度羽化的祖师,普度四方孤魂。普度活动有公普和私普之分,公普是以地方乡团祠庙为中心的大型祭祀,私普是个人和公司行号自行进行祭祀。照片为道场众人跪拜的场景。

On July 15th of the lunar calendar, Taoist temples conducted activities to pray for good weather, peace and prosperity. Fireworks were ignited in the evening, sutras were recited for the Taoist founder and to help release all souls from suffering. The activities might be held in private or in public. The public ones were larger, held at the ancestral hall of a local community. While the private ones were held by individuals or companies. The photo shows visitors of a Taoist temple worshipping on bent knees.

中秋拜月
The Mid-Autumn Festival

佚名 Unknown Photographer

农历八月十五为中秋节，始于唐朝初年，盛行于宋朝，至明清时已与元旦齐名。中秋节是中国三大灯节之一，也是一家团圆的日子。人们会回到家中团聚、赏月、祭祖。在老北京的风俗中，十五月圆时设"月光马"于庭，供以瓜果、月饼等品祭拜兔儿爷。照片为1940年前后中秋节儿童拜月的场景。

Dating back to the Tang Dynasty (618-907) and widely celebrated in the Song Dynasty (960-1279), the Mid-Autumn Festival, which falls on August 15th of the lunar calendar, became as well-known as New Year's Day in the Ming and Qing Dynasties (1368-1644, 1644-1911). As one of the three big lantern festivals, the Mid-Autumn Festival is an occasion of family reunion, during which people join their families in appreciating the moon and offering sacrifices to their ancestors. As a custom in Beijing, a table called "moonlight horse" would be put in their yard, on which there were fruits and moon cakes to show respect towards the Jade Hare, the moon god. The photo shows a boy worshipping the moon at the Mid-Autumn Festival around 1940.

风俗节令　　Customs and Festivals

婚礼迎亲队伍
The Bride Escort for a Wedding Ceremony

[德国] 赫达·莫里逊 [Germany] Hedda Morrison

中国古代称婚礼为昏礼，多在黄昏举行。程序一般包括：相亲、断八字、定聘、择日、送嫁、催嫁、迎亲、拜堂、出厅、闹洞房、回门。迎亲是传统婚姻习俗礼仪中最多姿多彩的部分。在结婚吉日，伴随着乐器的吹吹打打，穿着礼服的新郎会偕同媒人、亲友前往女家迎娶新娘。照片为在迎娶新娘路上的结婚队伍。

Chinese traditional weddings used to be called dusk ceremonies since they were mostly held at dusk. A wedding ceremony normally consisted of a blind date, checking the couple's zodiacs, betrothal, choosing a date, delivering the bride, urging to marry, escorting the bride, performing formal bows, leaving the hall, a rowdy party in the nuptial chamber and visiting the wife's parents. The bride escort is the most colorful part of the traditional wedding. On the day of wedding, the groom wearing a ceremonial dress accompanied by the matchmaker, relatives and friends would go with a band to the bride's home to carry her back. The photo shows a wedding escort on the way.

京 华 旧 影
Old Photos of Beijing

婚礼迎亲花轿
A Bridal Sedan Chair

佚名 Unknown Photographer

在迎亲的过程中，花轿是传统婚礼的核心，分为四人抬、八人抬两种，又有龙轿、凤轿之分。一般的轿队少则十几人，多则几十人，很是壮观。照片为1941年前后迎亲的八人抬花轿。

For a traditional wedding ceremony, a sedan chair in a bride escort was the core element. These chairs were carried by either four or eight persons, and also included a dragon or a phoenix chair (for grooms or bride). The number of members in an escort team ranged from a dozen to even dozens. The photo shows a bridal sedan chair carried by eight persons around 1941.

风俗节令　　Customs and Festivals

婚礼拜天地
Worshipping the Heaven and Earth

"拜堂"又称为"拜天地",即"一拜天地,二拜高堂,夫妻对拜"。拜天地代表着对天地神明的敬奉,拜高堂是对孝道的体现,夫妻对拜则代表夫妻相敬如宾。经过拜堂后,新娘就正式成为新郎家庭中的一员。正在拜堂的这对新人,新娘头戴特制的凤冠霞帔,身穿绣花长裙,佩戴花饰;新郎头戴礼帽,身着长袍马褂,是民国时期的代表性结婚礼服。

A worshipping ceremony includes the couple-to-be showing their respect to the heaven and earth, to their parents, and finally to each other. It represents traditional Chinese respect to gods, filial piety to parents, and the couple's love towards each other. The bride would officially become a member of the groom's family after this ceremony. The photo shows a couple worshipping the heaven and earth. The bride was wearing a phoenix coronet and robes of rank, a long embroidered skirt and flower-shaped decorations, on the other side, the groom was wearing a ceremonial hat and a long robe with a mandarin jacket. They were typical wedding costumes during the Republic of China period (1912-1949).

佚名 Unknown Photographer

集团婚礼
Group Wedding

1937年，为改进习俗，提倡节约，尊重婚礼起见，北平市社会局参照民间刚刚兴起的文明结婚仪式，曾举办"集团婚礼"。即若干对新婚夫妇在同一天、同一地点，在同一证婚人主持下，统一举行婚礼。首届集团婚礼是1937年6月20日在中南海怀仁堂举行的，新郎、新妇的礼服都是统一规定的。

In 1937, in order to reform old customs, promote thriftiness and respect the wedding ceremony, based on a new trend in wedding ceremonies among the general public, the Bureau of Civil Affairs of Beiping (the old name of Beijing) once held "group weddings". A group wedding means a certain number of newlyweds celebrate their weddings on the same day, in the same place, and with the same officiant presiding. The first group wedding was held at Magnanimity Hal in Zhongnanhai, on June 20th, 1937. At that time, the brides' and the grooms' costumes had to be uniformly decided.

佚名 Unknown Photographer

风俗节令　Customs and Festivals

出殡
Funeral Procession

佚名 Unknown Photographer

殡葬礼仪是中华民族传承下来的一种特殊风俗文化。流程通常包括小殓、报丧、奔丧、停灵、守灵、大殓、出殡与下葬、烧七、五七、守孝、牌位、扫墓等。出殡是葬礼的最后一幕，其仪仗加上送殡的孝属、亲友、车辆，浩浩荡荡，队伍一般长达三四里。其中，打雪柳是仪仗队伍中的重要组成部分，雪柳是丧家在灵前供奉或出殡时用作仪仗之物。在三四尺长的竹筒上插上裹了白纸穗子的细竹条，使之下垂，谓之雪柳，一般是12把，雪柳由穿孝服的男童手执，以壮大执事行列和场面。照片为出殡仪仗中男童打着雪柳。

As a very special custom handed down in Chinese culture, a traditional funeral ceremony is composed of washing and dressing the body, announcing the death, hastening home for a funeral, keeping the coffin in a temporary shelter, keeping vigil beside the coffin, putting the body into the coffin, carrying the coffin to the cemetery, burying the deceased, burning the ceremonial fires on designated days, observing the mourning, displaying the ancestral tablets, and sweeping the tombs. As the most crucial event of a funeral ceremony, the funeral procession was joined by family members, relatives, and friends. The procession could extend up to 2000 meters. "Snow Willows", made of thick bamboo tubes and stuck with bamboo splits, on which paper pieces were tied, were important ceremonial objects in the procession. Carried by young boys in white mourning gowns they were used to give the procession a spectacular look as the photo show.

京 华 旧 影
Old Photos of Beijing

丧礼——撒纸钱
Funeral—Scattering Paper Money

［德国］赫达·莫里逊 [Germany] Hedda Morrison

撒纸钱的风俗始于晚清。在死者出殡、移动棺材时，家属会将纸钱撒在道路、河川上，以供路上、河川的鬼神享用，避免刁难死者亡魂，是打发"外祟"和"拦路鬼"的买路钱。在出殡队伍中，孝子前面要有撒纸钱的人，途中经过十字路口、河沿、庙堂、井台、城门、桥梁以及入葬时，都要在杠前高高扬起纸钱。图为送葬出殡队伍经过电车轨道时向空中扬撒纸钱。

The custom of scattering paper money began in the late Qing Dynasty (1644-1911). When a coffin carrying the deceased left his or her home for the cemetery, family members scattered paper money onto the roads and rivers ahead of it. These so-called money were used to appease other souls along the procession path, so that they did not bother the dead. A person marching in front of the son of the deceased would be responsible for scattering the paper money. When passing crossings, river banks, temples, wells, city gates, bridges, and at the beginning of the burial, the person would spread the "money" into the air in front of the coffin. The photo shows the "money throwing" practice when a procession passed a tramway.

孙中山灵柩奉安
Dr. Sun Yat-Sun's Funeral

佚名 Unknown Photographer

1925 年 5 月 26 日凌晨 1 时，在哀乐和礼炮声中，孙中山的灵柩由 24 名杠夫抬出灵堂。中午 12 时，灵柩转入西长安街，3 时到达东车站被奉上火车。从碧云寺到东车站，沿途分段搭筑素彩牌楼，北京市各衙署、城门、牌坊均悬国旗、张素彩素灯，商店居民悬半旗，路旁瞻仰送殡群众达 30 万人。灵榇每经过一地，民众均自动脱帽，俯首肃立，各工厂汽笛每 10 分钟长鸣一次致哀。下午 4 时许，灵车从北京启程回南京。

At 1 am on the 26th of May, 1925, accompanied by funeral music and gun salute, Dr. Sun Yat-Sen's coffin was carried out of the mourning hall. At 12 o'clock, the coffin was transported to West Chang'an Avenue and carried onto the train at East Station at 3 pm. From Biyun Temple to the East Station, batches of white pailou (decorated archway) were established along the road. In Beijing, national flags and white lamps were hung on all government offices, gates and archways. Residents and shopkeepers hung flags at half-mast. More than 300 thousand people stood along the road with reverence for the funeral. Wherever the coffin passed, people took off their hats, bowed their heads, and stood in silent tribute. Sirens in all factories blew once every ten minutes to express condolences. Around 4 pm, the hearse departed from Beijing for Nanjing.

坐賈行商

Shops and Vendors

六必居
Liubiju

佚名 Unknown Photographer

六必居是北京老字号。相传始建于明嘉靖九年（1530），原为山西赵存仁兄弟三人开的杂货店，兼卖伏酒，后增添了酱菜生产。如今，六必居酱菜制作技艺已被列为国家级非物质文化遗产。照片为1936年六必居同仁合影。

As a time-honored brand in Beijing, Liubiju is said to be established in the 9th year of Jia Jing (1530) by a man named Zhao Cunren and his two brothers from Shanxi Province. It was originally a grocery store selling glutinous rice wine and later on pickled vegetables in soy sauce started to be produced. Nowadays, Liubiju's techniques in making pickled vegetables have been listed as National Intangible Cultural Heritage. The photo above taken in 1936 shows the staff of Liubiju.

天福号
Tianfuhao

佚名 Unknown Photographer

天福号始创于清乾隆三年（1738），由山东人刘凤翔经营，因无钱做匾，就买了一块"天福号"旧匾。天福号酱肘子以"肥而不腻，瘦而不柴，皮不回性，浓香醇厚"享誉京城，成为清宫贡品。天福号酱肘子制作技艺已列为国家级非物质文化遗产。

Established in the 3rd year of Qian Long (1738), Tianfuhao was operated by Liu Fengxiang from Shandong Province. Because lack of money for a new name board, he bought an old one with "Tianfuhao" inscribed on it, thus named his store after it. As a tribute to the royal court of the Qing Dynasty (1644-1911), Tianfuhao's spiced pork shoulder is famous for its good taste with both fat and lean meat and its production techniques have been listed as national intangible cultural heritage.

谦祥益
Qianxiangyi

佚名 Unknown Photographer

道光年间，山东谦祥益布店在北京前门设分店，1900年被烧毁，不久重建，在上海、天津等城市都有分店，北京谦祥益为总店。1949年后几经改名，后恢复谦祥益老字号，其建筑为北京市级文物保护单位。

In the reign of Emperor Dao Guang (1821-1850), Qianxiangyi Cloth Store originated in Shandong Province set up a branch in Beijing, which was rebuilt after being destroyed in a fire in 1900. There were branch stores in cities including Shanghai, Tianjin and so on, with the store in Beijing as the headquarter. After 1949, the name of the store was changed several times, in the end, the time-honored brand Qianxiangyi was restored. The store building is under protection as a Municipal Cultural Heritage Site of Beijing.

坐贾行商　　Shops and Vendors

瑞蚨祥
Ruifuxiang Silk and Cloth Shop

佚名 Unknown Photographer

北京瑞蚨祥绸布店始建于清光绪十九年（1893），由山东人孟雒川投资 8 万两白银。1900 年被烧毁。大灾之后，瑞蚨祥承诺：因账簿烧毁，欠客户的债务一律凭证奉还，客户欠瑞蚨祥的债务一笔勾销。在商界被传为佳话。火灾之后，仅用一年就在原址建起中西合璧的新店堂。瑞蚨祥坚持"至诚至上，货真价实，言不二价，童叟无欺"的经营宗旨，在海内外赢得好评。

Ruifuxiang was initially established in the 19th year of Guang Xu (1893) with an initial investment of 80,000 taels of silver by Meng Luochuan from Shandong Province. Although its account books were burned in a big fire in 1900, it promised to pay back its debts to all clients according to their certificates and that clients didn't need to pay their debts to Ruifuxiang. It's deed highly praised far and wide in the commercial circle. A new building combining eastern and western styles was built at its original place within only one year after the fire. The store adhered to the management principles of "sincerity, genuine goods at fair prices, no bargaining and honesty to every customer", which helped it earn a good reputation both at home and abroad.

荣宝斋
Rongbaozhai Stationery Studio

佚名 Unknown Photographer

荣宝斋的前身是松竹斋，始创于清康熙十一年（1672），店主姓张，初为南纸店，经营各种书画纸张、文房用品等。清朝末年，店主为重振松竹斋生意，聘请庄虎臣为经理，光绪二十年（1894）年改名荣宝斋，后在全国各地设分店，在全国同业中领先，其木板水印技艺更是闻名中外。

Rongbaozhai Shop, originally known as Songzhuzhai, was founded by a man with the family name of Zhang in the 11th year of the reign of Emperor Kangxi (1672) the Qing Dynasty (1664-1911), selling calligraphic works, paintings, paper and materials used in studies originally as a shop of paper produced in southern China. After the owner hired Zhuang Huchen as the manager to revive the business in the late Qing Dynasty, the shop was renamed as Rongbaozhai in the 20th year of the reign of Emperor Guangxu (1894). With branches all over the country, it was in the leading position in the industry for its well-known woodblock painting technique.

坐贾行商　　Shops and Vendors

文盛斋
Wenshengzhai

佚名 Unknown Photographer

文盛斋由浙江人娄逸亭、俞莲峰创建于清嘉庆十一年（1806），原是灯画扇店，以彩灯著名。1915年参加在美国举办的巴拿马太平洋万国博览会，获两枚金牌。产品远销欧美，出口宫灯为其重要业务。

Established in the 11st year of Jia Qing (1806) by Lou Yiting and Yu Lianfeng from Zhejiang Province, Wenshengzhai specialized in lanterns, paintings and fans, and was particularly famous for its colored lanterns. Winning two gold medals in the Panama Pacific International Exposition in the USA in 1915, it sold products to Europe and America with palace lanterns as the main export.

京 华 旧 影
Old Photos of Beijing

同仁堂
Tongrentang

佚名 Unknown Photographer

同仁堂，清康熙八年（1669）由曾任太医院吏目的浙江人乐显扬创建。其三子乐凤鸣传承父业，于康熙四十一年（1702）在大栅栏开设前店后厂的同仁堂药铺，收集整理祖传秘方，并立下了"炮制虽繁必不敢省人工，品味虽贵必不敢减物力"的宗旨。同仁堂中医药文化已列入国家级非物质文化遗产。

Tongrentang Pharmacy was founded in the 8th year of Kang Xi (1669) by Yue Xianyang from Zhejiang Province, who was an official in the Imperial Hospital. Yue's third son Yue Fengming inherited his father's business and set up Tongrentang Pharmacy and a processing factory in Dashilan area near Qianmen in 41 st year of Kangxi (1702). He collected and put in order the secret prescription handed down from the previous generations. He laid down a principle that never saving steps of efforts in processing medicine and never reduce expensive ingredients. Tongrentang's traditional Chinese medicine techniques have been listed as National intangible cultural heritage.

坐贾行商　　Shops and Vendors

大栅栏
Dashilan

[日本] 不动健治 [Japan] Kenji Hudowu

大栅栏原称廊房四条，与头、二、三条并列。明永乐以后，成为一条繁华街市。清乾隆年间，在廊房四条东口和西口，建起两座高大的木栅栏，以后大栅栏便成为街名。大栅栏不仅商店数量众多，商品种类齐全，而且还集中了一批老字号店铺。如同仁堂药店、马聚源帽店、瑞蚨祥绸缎庄、内联升鞋店、长和厚绒线铺等；这里的戏园子也比较多，有庆乐园、庆和楼、三庆园、广德楼、同乐轩等。

Dashilan was original named the Langfang Fourth Lane, along with the First, Second, and Third lanes. It became a prosperous business area at the beginning of the reign of Emperor Yong Le (1403-1424) of the Ming Dynasty. Under Emperor Qian Long's reign (1736-1795), two big (da) wooden railings (shilan) were installed at its western and eastern end, so the street was renamed Dashilan. It was famous for not only a complete range of goods, but also a lot of time-honored brands, like Tongrentang Pharmacy, Majuyuan Hattery, Ruifuxiang Silk Store, Neiliansheng Shoe Store and Changhehou Wool Shop. A lot of folk opera houses including Qingleyuan, Qinghelou, Sanqingyuan, Guangdelou and Tonglexuan were also established there.

[德国] 海因茨·冯·佩克哈默 [Germany] Heinz v. Perckhammer

坐 贾 行 商　　　　Shops and Vendors

东安市场
Dong'an Market

东安市场始建于清光绪二十九年 (1903)，因邻近东安门而得名。原为练兵场，1902年因清政府翻修东华门大街，将沿街摊贩全部迁到这里，到光绪末年，东安市场已成为北京内外城有名的繁华大市场。

Established in the 29th year of Guang Xu (1903), Dong'an Market was named after the nearby Dong'anmen. It originally served as a drilling ground for the army. In order to renovate the Donghuamen Street in 1902, the Qing court moved all vendors nearby to this place. By the end of Emperor Guang Xu's reign (1875-1908), the market had already become a famous and bustling shopping centre in the Inner and Outer City of Beijing.

佚名 Unknown Photographer

佚名 Unknown Photographer

东安市场不但摊店众多，百业杂陈，而且天天开放，交通便利，许多热衷"赶庙会"的北京人逐渐被吸引到市场里来。市场生意日渐兴隆。又经过多年发展和几次扩建，市场规模不断扩大，特别是接受了两次大火灾的教训，由商民公益联合会与市政公所共同规划，把各店门前原有的四尺走廊全部取消，拓宽中间人行路，路中设摊，两边各留"火道"既利于防火，又便于顾客活动。有些商店自己建起了楼房，几条主要街道都是两层楼房，并支搭了铁皮罩棚，场内路上铺上钢砖，形成了一个不怕风吹雨淋的室内市场。

With numerous shops offering all sorts of goods and convenient transportation, Dong'an Market attracted people interested in temple fair day after day, thus making the business here increasingly prosperous. It expanded gradually. Year by year, after two big fires, the Commonwealth Association of Businessmen and Urban Public Administration decided to replace the original narrow corridors with a wider pathway for passengers. Stalls were set up in the middle of the way, leaving enough place for customers to move around and be evacuated in case of fire. Some merchants built houses along the main streets, most of which were two storey buildings. Metal awnings were pitched and the roads in the market were paved with steel bricks, thus ensuring continuous operation even in a bad weather.

六国饭店
Liuguo Hotel

[日本] 岩田秀则 [Japan] Hidenori Iwata

佚名 Unknown Photographer

六国饭店由英国人于1905年建造，当初是英法美德日俄六国合资，所以名为六国饭店。六国饭店位于北京东交民巷核心区，是当时北京最高的洋楼之一。

Built in 1905 by British, Liuguo Hotel (Six Nations Hotel) was named because its construction was co-funded by England, France, America, Germany, Japan and Russia. Located in the core area of Dongjiaominxiang, it was one of the tallest western-style buildings in Beijing at that time.

北京饭馆楼上的雅座
Lounges at the Top of the Beijing Hotel

佚名 Unknown Photographer

跑堂的用托盘为楼上雅座送餐，一个托盘上三个火锅，平步上楼显功夫。

A waiter serving meals was climbing stairs with three hot spots on the tray, showcasing his excellent skills.

坐 贾 行 商　　Shops and Vendors

清华池
Qinghua Bathing Pool

佚名 Unknown Photographer

清华池始建于清光绪三十一年（1905），位于珠市口西大街，初名"小沧浪澡堂"，后经山东回民于子明改建，更名为"清真清华池"。后几经翻建，服务项目增多，以修脚最为著名。

Established in the 31st year of Guang Xu (1905) at Zhushikou West Street, Qinghua Bathing Pool was first named "Xiaocanglang Pond", and renamed "Muslim Qinghua Pond" after it was reconstructed by Yu Ziming, a Muslim man from Shandong Province. It was reconstructed several times, offering more services, among which pedicure was the most famous.

清华园
Qinghuayuan Bathing Pool

佚名 Unknown Photographer

清华园浴池位于王府井，原名东兴园浴池。1917年更名为清华园浴池。1931年在锡拉胡同开设全市第一家女浴所。

Located at Wangfujing and named firstly as Dongxingyuan Bathing Pool, Qinghuayuan got its current name in 1917. Qinghuayuan set up the first women's bathing pool of Beijing in Xila Hutong in 1931.

坐贾行商　　Shops and Vendors

繁华的东四牌楼大街
Prosperous Dongsipailou Street

[法国] 阿尔贝·杜帖特 [France] Albert Dutertre

东四牌楼大街，曾名大市街，是京城著名的商业街。民国三十六年（1947），十字路口以北改称东四北大街，以南改称东四南大街，并沿用至今。

Dongsipailou Street, once named Dashi Street (Big Market Street), was a famous shopping center in Beijing. The part to the north of the crossing was renamed Dongsi North Street and the part to the south was named Dongsi South Street in the 36th year of the Republic of China (1947) and both names are still in use.

阜成门外的煤栈
Coal Bunkers Outside of Fuchengmen

佚名 Unknown Photographer

阜成门，原为平则门，是明清两代自门头沟运煤进城的重要通道，故有"煤门"之称。在阜成门附近，设立了许多煤厂、煤栈、煤店，从事京西煤炭的转运、储存和贸易活动。

Originally named Pingzemen and nick-named the Coal Gate, Fuchengmen used to be an important passage way for transporting coal from Mentougou into the Inner City in the Ming and Qing Dynasties (1368-1644, 1644-1911). A lot of coal yards, bunkers and shops were set up around the Gate, running business such as coal transportation, storage and trade.

坐 贾 行 商　　Shops and Vendors

德元成棉花店
Deyuancheng Cotton Shop

佚名 Unknown Photographer

德元成位于正阳门外商业区，经营棉花的零售与批发业务。店门前悬挂的是这个行业特有的招幌。招幌形如灯笼，椭圆形的白色棉团，中腰缠一条红布带，下缀一条红布。

Located in the business area outside of Zhengyangmen, Deyuancheng Cotton Shop specialized in the retail and wholesale business of cotton. In front of the shop, there hanged a special shop sign, an oval-shaped white cotton ball with a red ribbon in the middle and a strip of red cloth hanging down, similar to a Chinese lantern.

杂货摊
Stalls Selling Sundry Goods

[日本] 岩田秀则 [Japan] Hidenori Iwata

杂货主要指以竹、木、草、羽毛等产自农村的自然原材料制作的生活日用品，也包括少量铁器和陶瓷制品。照片为花市大街上的杂货摊。

Sundry goods sold here include daily necessities made of natural materials from the villages like bamboo, wood, weeds or feathers, and some ironware and ceramics. The photo shows stalls at Huashi Street.

缸瓦杂货铺
Earthenware Groceries

[法国] 斯提芬·帕瑟 [France] Stephane Passet

"缸瓦"主要指日用陶器，包括粗砂陶器和施釉的细陶器，如锅、碗、盆、罐、缸等。老北京经营缸瓦杂货的摊铺很多，因经营缸瓦、陶器、瓷器的集市而得名的街道，称缸瓦市，位于西四南大街南侧。

Earthenware refers to potteries, including unglazed coarse and glazed refined ones such as pots, bowls, dishes, jars and vats. Because there were a lot of earthenware groceries in old Beijing, some streets were even named after them, such as Gangwashi (Earthenware Market Street) in the south of Xisi South Street.

京 华 旧 影
Old Photos of Beijing

竹柳器铺
Basketry

佚名 Unknown Photographer

竹柳器铺子在老北京四处可见，在崇文门外大街、宣武门外大街、花市、东四、隆福寺、护国寺一带都有，这些摊子上所卖的东西都是用竹、柳条和荆条编制的生活用品，这些铺子也被叫做筐篓铺。

Shops or stalls selling basketry could be seen everywhere in old Beijing, particularly at Chongwenmen Outer Street, Xuanwumen Outer Street, Huashi, Dongsi, Longfu Temple and Huguo Temple. The products sold at those stalls were mainly for daily use and were made of bamboo strips, willow twigs or chaste tree twigs, which was why the shops were also called basket shops.

琉璃厂古玩摊
Antique Stalls in Liulichang

琉璃厂位于北京南城和平门外。元明时期曾是皇家烧造琉璃建材的窑厂。清初以来南城成为文人士子集中居住之地，此地初现书市雏形。乾隆年间开馆修纂《四库全书》，进而发展成为一个集图书、古玩、文具、书画于一街的文化中心。民国以后在此开辟的"海王村公园"，亦为文化用品经营场所。

Located outside of Hepingmen in southern Beijing, Liulichang used to be a glazed tile (liuli) factory (chang) for the imperial court in the Yuan and Ming Dynasties (1271-1368, 1368-1644). At the beginning of the Qing Dynasty (1644-1911), it became a place where the literati got together and an early form of the book market emerged. Under the reign of Emperor Qian Long (1736-1795), the "Complete Library in the Four Branches of Literature" was compiled here, thus making Liulichang a center for books, antiques, stationery, calligraphies and paintings. During the Republic of China (1912-1949), Haiwangcun Park, also a market for stationery, was set up here.

佚名 Unknown Photographer

佚名 Unknown Photographer

坐 贾 行 商   Shops and Vendors

卖蛐蛐罐
Selling Cricket Tanks

佚名 Unknown Photographer

养蛐蛐是北京人的一种爱好。养蛐蛐讲究用蛐蛐罐。讲究的用澄泥罐，尺寸大的可达直径一尺，一般也有四五寸。罐底铺天然土以防烧蛐蛐。罐盖上塑有花草等各式花纹。

Many Beijingers were fond of keeping crickets in cricket pots, among which those made of clay are of the highest quality. Most pots were four or five cun (1/30 meter) in diameter and some may reach one chi (1/3 meter). Natural soil was laid on the bottom to keep inner environment cool and the cover was carved with patterns of flowers and grasses.

卖空煤油桶
Selling Empty Kerosene Tanks

佚名 Unknown Photographer

清中期中国开始使用煤油灯，1910年以后普及到普通人家。国外运来的煤油封装在长方形的铁皮桶中，使用过后，一些手艺人将其改制为铁壶、铁盆、铁盒等家庭日用品，或者用旧桶装上煤油以次充好二次售卖，于是就出现了专门从事收购后再转手出卖空煤油桶的买卖。

In the middle of the Qing Dynasty (1644-1911), kerosene lamps started to be used and became popular after 1910. The rectangular tanks carrying kerosene from abroad could be made into daily containers like iron pots, basins or boxesby craftsmen. They could also be refilled with substandard oil and sold again at the price of a new one. Therefore, people reselling used tanks started to emerge.

坐 贾 行 商　　　Shops and Vendors

卖灯笼的
A Woman Selling Lanterns

早年间在前门外大栅栏一带有专门卖灯的"灯局子",有宫灯、纱灯、羊角灯、玻璃灯,这些灯具精致价高。普通百姓多从走街串巷的卖灯笼人手里买灯笼,他们多是南城一带的贫困人家,自产自销,用秸秆编成各种形状的灯架,糊上高丽纸,涂上色彩,绘上人物、动物、花卉,有狮子灯、羊角灯、兔子灯、莲花灯、绣球灯等,颇受欢迎。

In the early years at the Dashilan area outside of Qianmen, there were some shops specializing in selling delicate and expensive lanterns, such as palace lanterns, horn-shaped lanterns and those made of gauze or glass. Ordinary people who could not afford them used to buy cheaper ones from street vendors, who were mostly poor people living in southern Beijing. They sold the products, which they made by themselves, by setting up the lamp skeletons with straw and gluing white paper on them. They drew colored figures, such as animals and flowers, making popular lanterns with lion, rabbit and lotus patterns and some in the shape of an embroidery ball or a horn.

佚名 Unknown Photographer

卖花的
A Man Selling Flowers

佚名 Unknown Photographer

佚名 Unknown Photographer

入夏后，北京街头卖鲜花的就多了起来。卖花的小贩挎着筐走街串巷。筐里放着应季的鲜花和小剪子、小钳子、细铜丝。卖花人用细铜丝穿制不同的鲜花，做成配饰，或者将鲜花做成室内摆放的装饰物，如花筒等。

When summer began, street vendors started to walk around the city to sell fresh flowers. They put fresh flowers, scissors, tweezers and copper wires in their baskets. With the copper wires, they pierced flowers together to create accessories and decorations ornamentals, such as flower vases.

坐 贾 行 商　　Shops and Vendors

卖金鱼的
A Man Selling Goldfish

佚名 Unknown Photographer

自金代起北京就有金鱼业。天桥以东有金代所凿的鱼藻池，以养金鱼为主，又名金鱼池。每年春天三四月间，胡同里也有卖小金鱼的，挑着带提梁的圆形木槽，里面放着各色金鱼、鱼苗、鱼虫或者玻璃鱼缸。嘴里吆喝着"大人小孩——喂小金鱼儿来哟"。

The goldfish business started in Beijing from the Jin Dynasty (1115-1234), when ponds were built to the east of Tianqiao to raise the fish. In March and April, goldfish vendors carrying wooden buckets on their shoulder could be seen everywhere, even in lanes, offering all sorts of goldfish, fish fries, water fleas and fishbowls. They shouted: "Hey everyone, come and feed little goldfish!"

京 华 旧 影
Old Photos of Beijing

风筝摊
A Kite Stall

佚名 Unknown Photographer

老北京风筝摊卖得最多的是沙燕，还有鹞子、刘海戏金蝉、蜈蚣等。老北京风筝可以分为两大家："风筝金"和"风筝哈"。金氏几代人在地安门大街的火神庙前摆风筝摊，哈氏几代人在琉璃厂开风筝铺。一北一南，各有特色。

The best-selling kites in old Beijing include swallow-shaped ones followed by the ones in the shape of sparrow hawks, golden toads and centipedes. Kites in old Beijing were mainly made by the Jin and the Ha family. The Jin family ran a kite stall for generations in front of the Huoshen Temple in Di'anmen Street, while the Ha family ran theirs at Liulichang, with both families having their own unique features. People flew kites based on festivals and customs.

卖噗噗噔的
Selling Pupudeng Toys

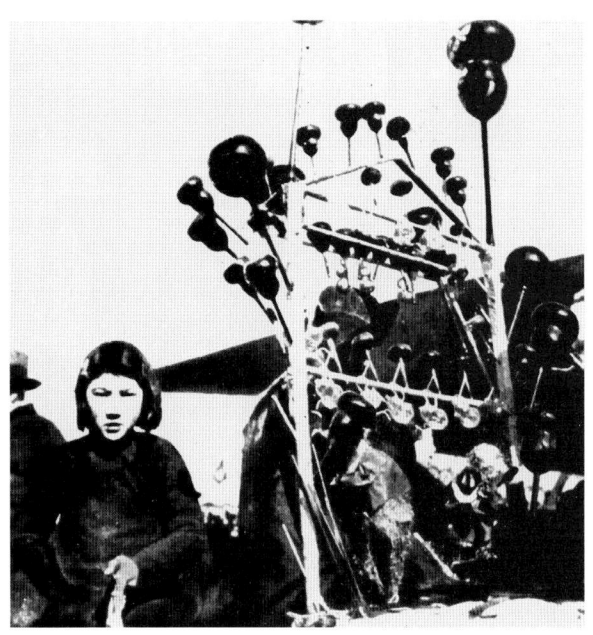 

佚名 Unknown Photographer

"噗噗噔儿"是用琉璃制作的音响玩具，照片中售卖的噗噗噔儿分为大小两种，其形如葫芦，小的直径约三寸，大的直径约一尺，颜色有白色透明、淡绿色、黄色。

Made of colored glaze, Pupudeng was a toy which can make noise. The photo shows a stall selling the toys, including small ones which has three cun (1/30 meter) in diameter and big ones which has one chi (1/3 meter) in diameter with varying colors including light green and yellow, as well as transparent ones.

京 华 旧 影
Old Photos of Beijing

卖鸡毛掸子的
A Man Selling Feather Dusters

[德国] 赫达·莫里逊 [Germany] Hedda Morrison

鸡毛掸子过去是家家户户的日常必需品。老北京走街串巷的小买卖有"八不语"的说法，"卖掸子"就是其中之一。因为"买掸子"与"卖胆子"谐音，叫卖出来不好听。后来就吆喝"大小掸子发行价"，一来以示便宜，二来告诉买主，卖掸子的来了。

Feather dusters used to be a daily necessity for every family. In old Beijing, sellers for eight products had no slogans, and the feather duster vendors was one of them. In Chinese, "buying dusters" and "selling courage" are the same pronunciation, so smart vendors changed the slogan into "selling big and small dusters at sale prices" to attract buyers.

"打瓢" 小贩
A Vendor Playing A Gourd Ladle

佚名 Unknown Photographer

"打瓢"小贩肩挑担子，挂满各种日用杂品，如鸡毛掸子、刷子、篦子、勺、扫帚等，像个流动的杂货铺。一般这种小贩不吆喝，而是用小棍敲一个掏空的半截葫芦，于是人们管这种小贩叫"打瓢"的。

A vendor selling feather dusters, brushes, combs, spoons, brooms and other daily necessities could attract customers by knocking at hollowed gourd with a little wooden stick instead of shouting. Therefore, they were called "gourd players".

京 华 旧 影
Old Photos of Beijing

永定门外小吃摊
A Food Stand Outside Yongdingmen

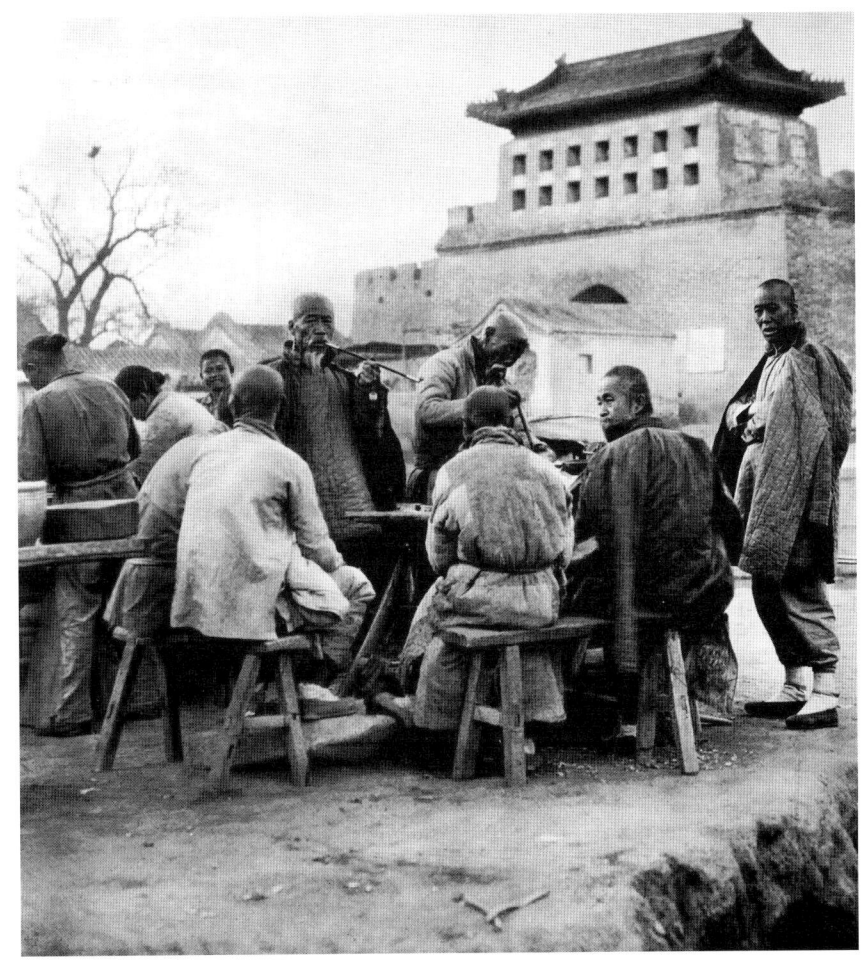

[英国] 唐纳德·曼尼 [Britain] Donald Mennie

北京小吃历史悠久，博采各地小吃之精华，兼收汉、回、满、蒙各民族小吃的风味及明清宫廷小吃的特点。北京小吃品种可谓丰富多彩，北京城内有许多著名的小吃街，还有许许多多的城边小吃摊。照片为永定门外的小吃摊，摊主正忙着给人盛小吃。

Time-honored Beijing snacks borrowed flavors from those of the Han, Hui, Manchu and Mongol nationalities and from those in the royal court of the Ming and Qing Dynasties (1368-1644, 1644-1911). Beijing had quite a few famous snack streets and even more cookshops at the fringe of the city, selling a variety of food. The photo shows a food stand outside Yongdingmen where the owner was busy serving customers.

坐 贾 行 商　　Shops and Vendors

什刹海荷花市场上的小吃摊
Food Stands at the Lotus Market at Shichahai

[法国] 斯提芬·帕瑟 [France] Stephane Passet

什刹海位于地安门桥西。民国五年（1916），什刹海开设了荷花市场，每年农历五月初一至七月十五，湖畔商贩云集，游人如梭。荷花市场的小吃摊盛极一时，夏天多以冷食为主，凉糕、扒糕、凉粉卖得最快。

Shichahai is Located at the west of Di'anmen Bridge. In the 5th year of the Republic of China (1916), a Lotus Market was established at Shichahai from May 1st to July 15th of the lunar calendar, with numerous shops alongside the lake attracting crowds of people. Among the snacks, cold snacks in the summer were most popular, including glutinous rice cakes, buckwheat cakes and mungbean jelly.

面条店
A Noodle Shop

[美国] 西德尼·D·甘博 [America] Sidney D. Gamble

挂面都是手工制作，将面团搓成条状，并用竹竿串挂在面杆上，隔几分钟拉拽一次，最后把细如银丝的面条晒干，切成五六寸长，用红绿彩纸裹好，论斤售卖。此照是源兴斋挂面庄晾晒挂面的场景。

Dried noodles in China were made by hand from noodle dough which was rubbed into stripes hung up on bamboo poles for drying. The stripes had to be stretched a bit every few minutes until they were as fine as silver wires. After they were finally dried under sunshine, they were cut into pieces five to six cun (1/30 meter) long, wrapped in red and green paper, and sold in the market. The photo shows drying noodles at the Yuanxingzhai Noodle Shop.

坐贾行商　　Shops and Vendors

豆汁摊
A Stall for Fermented Bean Soup

佚名 Unknown Photographer

豆汁是一种典型的北京风味小吃。据说始于辽代，流传至今已有一千多年的历史。

As a typical local Beijing drink, fermented bean soup was said to originate from the Liao Dynasty (907-1125), with a history of over a thousand years.

煎饼摊
A Pancake Stall

[美国] 西德尼·D·甘博 [America] Sidney D. Gamble

《宛平县志》记载，二月初二是"龙抬头日"。在这天吃煎饼是为了"引龙以出，且使百虫伏藏也"。煎饼摊不喜群居，而在偏僻的街边歇脚。一辆两轮人力平板车上覆之以平板，一头下坐火炉，火炉上搁一铁鏊子，铁鏊子黑黢黢泛着油光；另一头搁鸡蛋、油条、香葱、芝麻、香油之类。

According to the *Wanping County Records*, February 2nd of the lunar calendar is the "Dragon-Head-Raising Day" (*long tai tou*). Eating pancakes on that day is to "draw the dragon forth and intimidate hundreds of insects". People who sold pancakes did not like to stay in groups, they preferred to operate in remote and quiet places. The owner may put a board on the bicycle trolley, with a stove under one side and a black and glossy griddle on the stove; on the other side of the board, there were eggs, fried bread sticks, chives, sesame, and sesame oil, etc.

坐贾行商　　Shops and Vendors

卖大碗茶的
A Man Selling Big Bowls of Tea

佚名 Unknown Photographer

卖大碗茶的多是半大孩子和老头，他们挑着的挑子，一头是短嘴、大肚的绿釉大茶壶；另一头是荆条篮子，篮子上盖着布，布下是几个粗瓷大碗，有的还准备几个小板凳。

Most sellers of big bowl tea were elder children or old men, they carried poles on their shoulders, with a big green-glazed teapot with a short spout on one end and a cloth-covered wicker basket on the other end. With several big and stoneware bowls in the basket, some sellers even prepared small stools for customers.

送蜜供
Bringing Migong Snacks

[法国] 阿尔贝·杜帖特 [France] Albert Dutertre

蜜供是蘸了蜜糖的一种糕点，老北京敬神、佛、祖先上供的供品之一。此照为崇文门内大街上送蜜供的挑夫。

As a type of snack food covered by honey, Migongs were used by Beijing people as a typical offering to gods, the Buddha or ancestors. The photo shows a seller delivering Migongs in Chongwenmen Inner Street.

卖甜瓜的
A Man Selling Muskmelons

[日本] 岩田秀则 [Japan] Hidenori Iwata

北京人管香瓜叫甜瓜。其种类很多，有苹果青、三白、羊角蜜、蛤蟆酥等。甜瓜论个卖，主顾买好以后，小贩先用毛巾把瓜擦干净，然后划开看瓤儿，生了管换。

Called sweet melons by Beijing people, muskmelons could be classified into different varieties. They were sold one by one. After a customer paid, a vendor would clean it with a towel, cut it open to check if it is ripe. If it is not, the vendor would give the customer a new one.

京 华 旧 影
Old Photos of Beijing

卖年糕的
A Man Selling Rice Cakes

佚名 Unknown Photographer

北京的年糕是清真小吃，也是满族拜神用的祭品，满族名字叫"飞石黑阿峰"。北京的年糕，用黄米或江米面加各种辅料蒸制而成，品种多样，有枣年糕、豆年糕、年糕坨等。北京的年糕为北方年糕的代表，有黄、白两色，象征金、银，并有"年年高"的吉祥如意的寓意。

As a halal snack, rice cakes were also used by Manchu people as a sacrificial offering and are referred to as "Feishiheiafeng". Made of glutinous rice and a variety of ingredients, the cakes in Beijing could be classified into different types including jujube, bean or roll-shaped cakes. As the representative of rice cakes in Northern China, Beijing cakes could be divided into yellow and white ones, symbolizing gold and silver which were used as currency with an auspicious meaning of making progress in the New Year.

坐 贾 行 商　　Shops and Vendors

卖水果的
A Man Selling Fruits

[英国] 约翰·汤姆逊 [Britain] John Thomson

旧时京城卖水果的，有摆摊售卖的，也有挑着挑子走街串巷卖的。挑挑的一般都是自己家种的，到城里来卖。

In Old Beijing, fruits were sold in two ways, either at a market stall or by street vendors with a carrying pole walking through the lanes. The fruits they offered were mostly cultivated at the vendor's home and brought to the city.

卖酸梅汤的
A Man Selling Sweet-sour Plum Juice

佚名 Unknown Photographer

酸梅汤是北京一种传统的夏令清凉饮料，用乌梅加冰糖并点以桂花等熬制而成。每至盛夏，摊售者支起大布伞，案子用蓝布围起来，上面嵌着用白布剪成的"冰镇梅汤"四字。串街卖酸梅汤的，则用两个小铜盏相击发出的悦耳声音来招徕顾客。制售酸梅汤的店铺，以前门九龙斋、西单牌楼邱家和琉璃厂的信远斋最为有名。

As a traditional cold drink in Beijing in summer, plum syrup was made by boiling smoked plums, rock candy and sweet-scented osmanthus together. In midsummer, vendors set up big cloth umbrellas covered long tables with blue cloth, on which there were four characters "Bing zhen mei tang" (ice-cold plum syrup). Vendors walking around in the city chimed two copper bells to produce a pleasant sound to attract customers. The most famous shops selling such drink were the Jiulongzhai at Qianmen, the Qiu familiy at Xidan and the Xinyuanzhai at Liulichang.

卖大蒜的
A Garlic Seller

[德国] 海因茨·冯·佩克哈默 [Germany] Heinz v. Perckhammer

大蒜是人们日常生活中不可缺少的调料。采收蒜头时，把蒜秧子与大蒜一起编成辫子一样，三十头左右为一辫，成品就叫做蒜辫、也叫蒜辫子。然后架干晾晒至七八成干的时候再储存或者销售。用这种方法储存大蒜，蒜辫子中的大蒜不易失去水分。时至今日，人们依然采用这种办法储存、销售大蒜。

Garlic is an indispensable condiment in daily life. People braided around thirty pieces of garlics together by the stems after harvest. The products were sold after they were 70% to 80% dried on shelves. This way of keeping moisture in the garlics is still in use today.

卖白薯的
A Man Selling Sweet Potatoes

[日本] 岩田秀则 [Japan] Hidenori Iwata

在老北京，入冬之后就有卖烤白薯的。用铁桶做成炉腔，内生火炉，把入过窖的好白薯放在炉里的架上烘烤，隔一段时间翻一下，烤熟之后取出，用小笤帚刷去表面的浮土，揭皮露瓤，香味诱人，冬天里买一块烤白薯捧着吃还可以暖手。白薯除了烤着卖，也有蒸着卖的。

Roasted sweet potatoes were sold in winter in old Beijing, and were made of high-quality sweet potatoes stored in cellars. Raw potatoes were roasted on gridirons in furnace chambers which were made from metal buckets before they were turned over from time to time. When baked thoroughly, they were taken out and the dust on them was cleaned with a little whisk broom. They were sweet and delicious after they were peeled off. They could keep you warm if you hold one in your hand in a cold winter. Except being roasted, sweet potatoes could also be steamed before being sold.

坐 贾 行 商　　Shops and Vendors

二手地摊
A Stall of Second Hand Goods

[德国] 赫达·莫里逊 [Germany] Hedda Morrison

二手地摊，卖的都是旧货。旧时北京的小市就有很多卖旧货的，小市其实就是"晓市"，黎明拂晓之时交易的市场，又叫"鬼市"。崇文门外叫东小市，宣武门外叫西小市，德胜门外还有一处小市。

Stalls selling used goods could be found in dawn markets which were also referred to as ghost market due to its trading time. The one outside of Chongwenmen was called the Eastern Dawn Market and the one outside of Xuanwumen the Western Dawn Market, and there was another dawn market outside of Deshengmen.

京 华 旧 影
Old Photos of Beijing

兑换洋元
Currency Exchange

佚名 Unknown Photographer

过去银元和铜元并用，银元是大值货币，铜元是小值货币。北京街头上兑换钱的小摊一般是以零换整，以铜元兑换银元。过去银元的种类很多，各种银元的含银量不同，所值铜元的多少也就不一样，加上当时市场上的行情经常变化，兑换银元的小摊可以获取差价。照片中的小摊，除了兑换洋元，还同时经营着"寄卖东鸿记茶叶""哈德门香烟"等买卖。"洋元兑换"上面写着一行英文，其中"EXCHANGE（交换）"一词的字母"G"明显写倒了。

In the past, silver coins with big denomination and copper coins with smaller denomination were both in use. Money exchanging stalls normally helped customers change copper coins into silver ones. With different amounts of metal in different types of silver coins which were all in circulation and the changing markets, money exchangers could make profits from buying and selling coins. The stall in the photo also sold tea and cigarettes besides converting currencies. There is a line of English above the Chinese words of currency exchange, with the G in the word EXCHANGE written upside down.

坐 贾 行 商　　Shops and Vendors

算命先生
A Fortune-teller

[德国] 赫达·莫里逊 [Germany] Hedda Morrison

算命先生曾经在老北京的街头巷尾随处可见，每逢隆福寺、护国寺、白塔寺的庙会日，他们也都前去赶庙设摊。算命先生常见的有"算卦""相面""看风水"几种。

Seen everywhere in streets in old Beijing, fortune-tellers could also be found in the fair at Longfu, Huguo or White Pagoda Temples. The services they provided included practicing divination, reading the physiognomy and practicing geomancy.

长城上的摊贩
Vendors on the Great Wall

佚名 Unknown Photographer

这张照片展现的是在长城上准备向游客兜售纪念品的小贩。

A vendor selling souvenirs to tourists on the Great Wall.

市井生活

The Daily Life of Ordinary People

染房
A Dyer

佚名 Unknown Photographer

染房，又叫染坊。唐朝已盛行，在旧时北京很普遍，北京也出现了与染房有关的地名或者胡同，如蓝靛厂，又如以魏家染纺命名的魏染胡同等。照片为染房在晾晒刚刚染好的布。

Dyers, also called dye houses were already commonly seen in the Tang Dynasty (618-907) and could be seen everywhere in old Beijing. Some places or hutongs (alleyways) were even named after them, like Landianchang (indigo dyer), or Weiran Hutong, named after Wei's Dye House. The photo shows fabrics hung up after dyeing.

市井生活　The Daily Life of Ordinary People

席铺
A Mat Shop

佚名 Unknown Photographer

席铺又叫席箔铺，老北京的席铺各处皆有，尤以宣武门外大街为最多。席铺门口一般放一卷席或花栅儿做招幌。照片为自利成席铺的工人正在编织席子，旁边有一卷打广告的席子。

Mat shops, also called bamboo mat shops, were very common in old Beijing, with most of them located at Xuanwumen Outer Street. Shop owners used a rolled-up mat or a grate as a sign in front of their shops. The photo shows workers of Zilicheng Mat Shop weaving mats, with a mat nearby serving as an advertisement.

京 华 旧 影
Old Photos of Beijing

打竹帘的
Making Bamboo Curtains

佚名 Unknown Photographer

"打竹帘子哟"、"修理竹帘子",每逢夏日旧京的胡同里都会有这样的高声吆喝声。旧时人们因多年形成的节俭传统习俗,四合院大杂院的百姓人家使用的竹帘子,要延续用十几年或一两代人,当残损时仍舍不得丢弃,常让修理帘子的工匠进行修整,然后继续使用。

Shouting "making bamboo curtains" or "repairing bamboo curtains" could be heard every summer in the lanes of old Beijing. Ordinary people would ask craftsmen to repair their broken bamboo curtains, which they may use for decades over one or two generations.

市 井 生 活　　The Daily Life of Ordinary People

送水的
Water Delivery

[日本] 岩田秀则 [Japan] Hidenori Iwata

老北京人喝的水主要来自井水，城内大多数水井都是苦水井，甜水井少。这些甜水井大都归个人所有，雇人给附近各家送水。在老北京，这些地方被叫做"水窝子"。送水者一般用独轮车、人力或畜力双轮车运水，还建有储水的水房。送水的除收取水费外，还以三大节的"节礼"，冬日雪后的"酒钱"等形式，向主顾讨要报酬。

The people in old Beijing mainly got their drinking water from wells in the past. However, most of the well water in the city tasted bitter, while a small number of sweet wells was mostly owned by individuals. Therefore, those well owners hired people to deliver water from the so called "water nests" to the neighboring families on wheelbarrows or on manpowered or animal-powered two-wheelers. Water storage facilities were also built. Other than water fees, the deliverers asked for "festival present" during the three most important festivals and "liquor money" after a winter snow.

锔碗的
A Bowl Mender

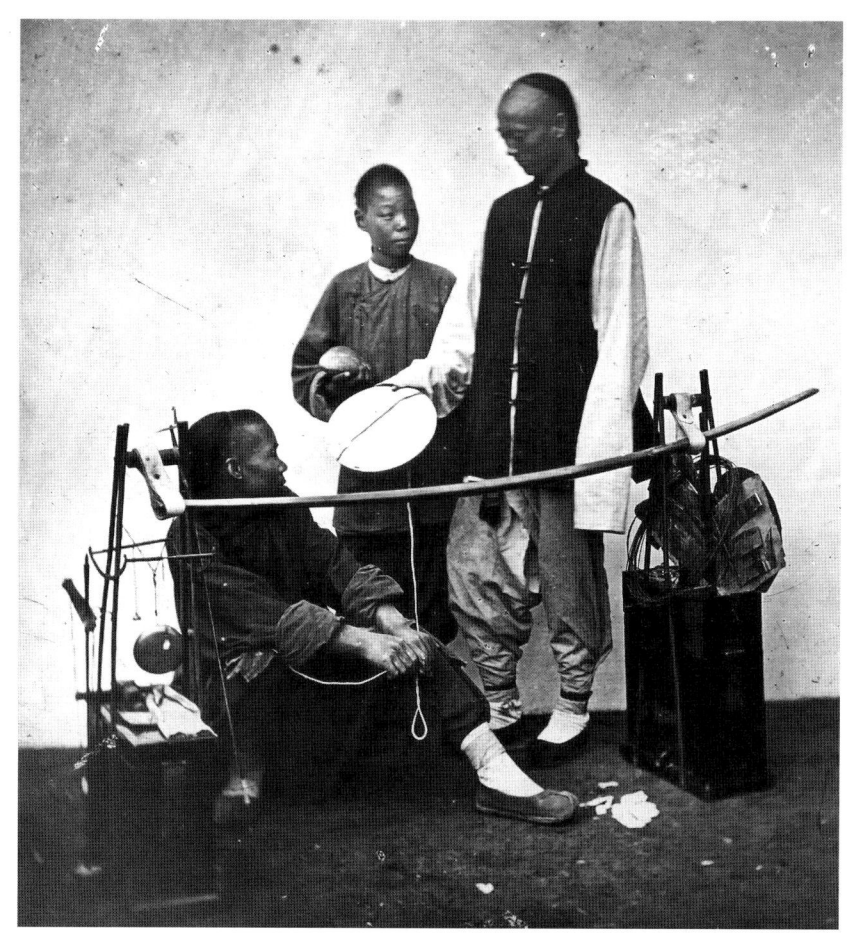

[英国] 约翰·汤姆逊 [Britain] John Thomson

老北京的普通百姓生活很节俭，生活用品坏了舍不得扔，修修补补再用，于是出现一种行当，人们称之为"锔碗的"，过去在老北京的街头巷尾常常可以遇到挑着担子的这种工匠，从事这个行业的人手很灵巧。壶、锅、碗、盆等破损了，都可以锔补。

Leading a frugal life, common people in old Beijing had a demand for mending their kettles, pots, bowls and dishes, because they couldn't afford to buy new ones. Therefore, a type of craftsmen called "bowl menders" emerged. By walking around with shoulder poles holding their tools, these skillful craftsmen could repair almost every type of household container.

市 井 生 活　　　The Daily Life of Ordinary People

芦苇秸秆编织
Weaving with Reed and Straw

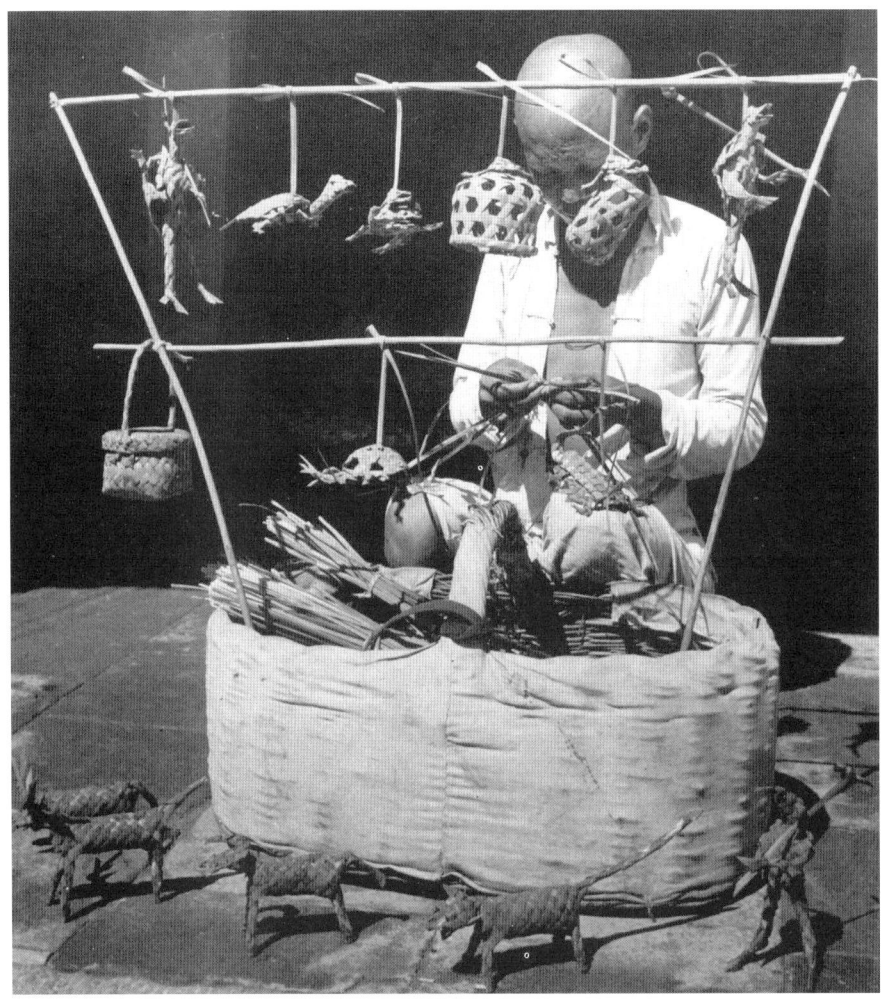

[德国] 赫达·莫里逊 [Germany] Hedda Morrison

编织艺人面前的篮子里放满了芦苇、秸秆，正在进行现场编织。架子上是他已经编织好的作品，有蝈蝈笼、造型各异的挂件。地面上还有很多编好的栩栩如生的小动物。

The photo shows an artisan weaving an item with a basket, full of reeds and straws in front of him. He showed his works such as grasshopper cages and pendants of different shapes on a shelf and life-like animal creations on the ground.

修脚的
Pedicure

[英国]约翰·汤姆逊 [Britain] John Thomson

修脚是治疗脚病的民间传统服务技艺。从业者民间称为"修脚匠",修脚匠有在浴池服务的,行话称为"画皮的",还有在街头(包括庙会、集市)行艺的,行话叫"剜窝的"。传统的修脚业,因手法、刀技的不同可分三大派:以北京为中心的河北派,以济南为中心的山东派,以扬州为中心的江苏派。

As a traditional skill to cure foot diseases, pedicure was practiced in public bathhouses, in the streets (including temple fairs and markets). Practitioners were called "pedicure craftsmen" with nicknames of "skin painter" if they were in public bathhouses and "foot fossa cutter" for those who on the street and at fairs. Based on the different techniques and knife techniques, the craft could be divided into three schools: the Hebei school in Beijing, the Shandong school in Jinan and the Jiangsu school in Yangzhou.

磨剪子磨刀
Grinding Knives and Scissors

[法国] 阿尔贝·杜帖特 [France] Albert Dutertre

磨剪子磨刀的手艺人绝少群聚，都是形单影只在街巷游走，吆喝着"磨剪子来，戗菜刀"。有的还吹一把小铜号，有的摇着四块铁板。照片为大阮府胡同内的一个磨剪子磨刀匠。

Generally working alone, craftsmen grinding knives and scissors walked around, chanting their business slogan. Some even blew a little brass horn or made noises with four little iron plates. The photo shows a knife grinder at Daruanfu Hutong.

剃头梳辫子
Barbering and Hair Braiding

[日本] 岩田秀则 [Japan] Hidenori Iwata

旧时剃头的多为挑担流动服务，在固定处所营业者不多。剃头匠挑担游走于街市之间，手执唤头，串走胡同，每到大街，将挑放在地上，等待来往之人刮脸、打辫子、剃头，方便之至。剃头是手艺活，老北京的剃头匠必须会16种技能，即梳、编、剃、刮、捏、拿、捶、按、掏、剪、剔、染、接、活、舒、补。

With only a few running their shops, barbers in the past normally walked around to deliver services in cities, by carrying their tools on their shoulders and ringing a bell to attract clients. When they came to a main street, they would choose a place to settle down and wait for customers to come. Barbering was an advanced skill, because the barbers in old Beijing had to master 16 different skills, namely, combing, braiding, shaving, scraping, pinching, holding, pounding, massaging, cleaning, cutting, trimming, dyeing, hair extending, bone setting, massaging and supplementing.

市 井 生 活　　The Daily Life of Ordinary People

摇煤球的
Making Coalballs

佚名 Unknown Photographer

居家过日子，做饭取暖烧开水，都需要煤球。摇煤球又脏又累，还要一定手艺，所以多数人家就雇请"摇煤球的"伙计代劳。老北京经营煤炭行业的大多是河北省定兴县人。"摇煤球的"先打扫出一片空地，然后和煤、摊晒、剁块儿、摇滚，最后晾干、苫好。

Cooking, heating or boiling water in daily life all required burning coalballs. Making coalballs was an exhausting, dirty and skillful job, so most Beijing people paid others, mostly those who from Dingxing County of Hebei Province, to do the job. After clearing a small place on the ground, coalball makers mixed coal powder with earth and water, dried the mixture, cut it into small pieces, rolled them into balls, and finally covered them carefully after drying.

市 井 生 活　　The Daily Life of Ordinary People

卖头饰的
Selling Headgears

[英国]约翰·汤姆逊 [Britain]John Thomson

满族妇女头上戴有头饰，老北京贩卖头饰是一个很赚钱的行当。从照片中满族妇女的穿着来看，应该是富裕人家的妇女。

Manchu women wore head ornaments on their heads. Selling head ornaments was a very profitable business. Looked at the dress of the Manchu women in the picture, these women should come from wealthy families.

钉马掌的
Horse-Shoeing

佚名 Unknown Photographer

早年间，骡马是主要的交通运输工具。钉马掌主要是为了保护骡马的蹄子免受损伤。在北京的城门附近、大道沿途的村边经常可以看到钉马掌的马掌铺。有的是铁匠铺兼钉马掌，也有是专门钉马掌的。

As the main means of transportation in the past, mules and horses had to be shoed to protect their hooves from getting hurt. Shops for shoeing horses could be found near city gates and in villages along main roads. Some shopkeepers were also blacksmiths while others only specialized in shoeing horses.

纺线织布
Spinning and Weaving

佚名 Unknown Photographer

崇文门外大街东侧的上四条胡同口，是北京有名的棉线店铺集中处。这里有德祥益、德泉、道德成等多家棉线庄，曾经藏在深闺中的女性开始学习纺线织布技艺，走出家门自食其力。

At the entrance of Shangsitiao Hutong, east to the Chongwenmen Outer Street there were a lot of shops selling cotton threads, including famous brands like Dexiangyi, Dequan, Daodecheng, etc. The photo shows women who used to stay at home learning thread-spinning and weaving to earn their own living.

京 华 旧 影
Old Photos of Beijing

木匠
Carpenter

[美国] 西德尼·D·甘博 [America] Sidney D. Gamble

老北京的木匠行分工细致，有大木行、细木行、车匠、家具行、杂木行、斜木行等。大木行专注于传统房屋木结构，细木行专注于传统房屋细部，车匠以造车为主，家具行以造传统家具为主，斜木行则是做棺材的。

在木匠行中，最低等的是串街修理的木工，不称匠，一般来说，木匠手艺一下街，也就不值钱了，因为没有专业分工，有什么活干什么活，用户也是看价格不看技术，从业者只能卖力气挣辛苦钱。

Carpentry in old Beijing had a detailed division of labor, including big carpentry, the making of the wooden structure of traditional houses, detailed carpentry for windows and doors, and carpentry for carts, furniture and coffins.

The carpenters who repaired things by walking around in neighborhoods were at the lowest level of the trade. They were not specialized only did repairs and thus could not earn a decent salary as craftsmen, because what customers needed from them was only cheap and simple work, instead of skills. Therefore, those carpenters could only earn their living through manual labor.

市 井 生 活　　The Daily Life of Ordinary People

胡琴制作
Making Huqin

佚名 Unknown Photographer

京 华 旧 影
Old Photos of Beijing

胡琴是中国传统乐器中的大众化乐器，胡琴伴随着京剧的普及也广为流传。胡琴的用料以及制作十分讲究，有名的琴师会招聘工人制作和销售胡琴，其中"马良正"是当时最著名的胡琴铺。照片拍摄于北京打磨厂的乐器店，工人们正在打磨制造胡琴的弓和琴体。

As a two-stringed bowed instrument, Huqin became very popular together with the development of Peking Opera. Famous huqin makers employed workers to make and sell such instruments which are made of high-end materials with superb skills, thus giving birth to famous Huqin shops, like "Ma Liangzheng", a well-known one in old Beijing. The photo shows the workers manufacturing and polishing the body and bows of Huqin in a shop in Damochang of Beijing.

市 井 生 活　　The Daily Life of Ordinary People

琉璃瓦制作
Making Glazed Tiles

北京琉璃渠窑厂自元代就是皇家的官窑，一直按朝廷工部规制烧制琉璃瓦构件，形成了中国皇家建筑标准的琉璃瓦制作流程。一件琉璃制品从原料到烧制成品需要十多天的时间，包括原料的粉碎、淘洗、配料、炼泥、制坯、修整成型、烘干、素烧、施釉、二次入窑烧釉、出窑等二十多道工序。

The Beijing Liuliqu Kiln had already been the official kiln for the royal family since the Yuan Dynasty (1271-1368). Following the order of the Manufacturing Department in the imperial court to produce the encaustic tiles, the factory set the Chinese royal standards of manufacturing encaustic tiles. It took about ten days to turn raw materials into one colored glaze product via more than 20 steps, including ingredient smashing, elutriating, dosing, mud-refining, tile mold trimming and shaping, stoving, biscuiting, glazing, gloss firing, drawing, etc.

佚名 Unknown Photographer

佚名 Unknown Photographer

市 井 生 活　　The Daily Life of Ordinary People

地毯制造
Making Carpets

北京的手工织毯有着悠久的历史，元代以来北京先后出现一些织造宫毯的作坊，到了清咸丰时期，西藏的织毯工匠纷纷进驻京城，手工织毯迅速兴盛繁荣起来。达官显贵们更是视自家府邸能够铺上宫毯为荣耀。清朝后期，北京织毯的样式不断更新，织毯工匠为满足官宦之家、生意人及文人雅士的需求，花费心思织造出各种新品，民间作坊百家争鸣，地毯样式层出不穷，毯面的构图日益多元化；普通百姓家中也逐渐铺毯。

The time-honored business of making carpets by hands started in workshops manufacturing carpets for the royal family in the Yuan Dynasty (1271-1368), and prospered after Tibetan carpet artisans flooded into the capital during the reign of Emperor Xianfeng (1851-1862) of the Qing Dynasty (1644-1911). Dignitaries considered it an honor to be able to have such a carpet at home. During the later Qing Dynasty (1644-1911), craftsmen spared no effort in creating new carpets to meet the demand of government officials, businessmen and scholars. With flooded thriving workshops which competed with each other and the diversification of shapes and patterns, these carpets gradually arrived at the houses of common people.

佚名 Unknown Photographer

市 井 生 活　　The Daily Life of Ordinary People

景泰蓝制作
Making Cloisonné

[英国] 约翰·汤姆逊 [Britain] John Thomson

景泰蓝，北京著名的汉族传统手工艺品，距今已有 600 多年的历史。又称"铜胎掐丝珐琅"，俗名"珐蓝"，因其在明朝景泰年间盛行，制作技艺比较成熟，使用的珐琅釉以蓝色为主，故而得名"景泰蓝"。照片为北京景泰蓝制作的场景。

Cloisonné (Jingtai blue) is one of the most famous traditional handicrafts of the Han nationality in Beijing, with a history of more than six hundred years. Cloisonné is also called "filigree enamel with copper body", commonly known as "falan". Since it was popular during the Jingtai Reign (1450-1457) of the Ming Dynasty (1368-1644), and its craftsmanship was well-developed and the enamel glaze used by this handicraft mainly blue, it was named "Jingtai blue". This is a picture showing the process of making Cloisonné in Beijing.

绕线的
Thread-Spinning

[德国] 赫达·莫里逊 [Germany] Hedda Morrison

线是由单股的丝绵、毛线等合股而成，单股的丝棉只能称为"线披"或作"坯"，两根合股后才能称之为"线"，合股后的线才能使用。合线的工匠又称"索线的"。过去在没有机器的情况下，都是手工将单股的丝绵、毛线进行合股。

Threads were made of single pieces of wool or silk floss, which were called basic materials. Two pieces of flosses could only be put into use after they were wound together into a piece of thread. The craftsmen who wind the thread was called the "thread winder". Without machines, craftsmen had to wind them together by hand.

吹糖人的
Blowing Sugar Figurines

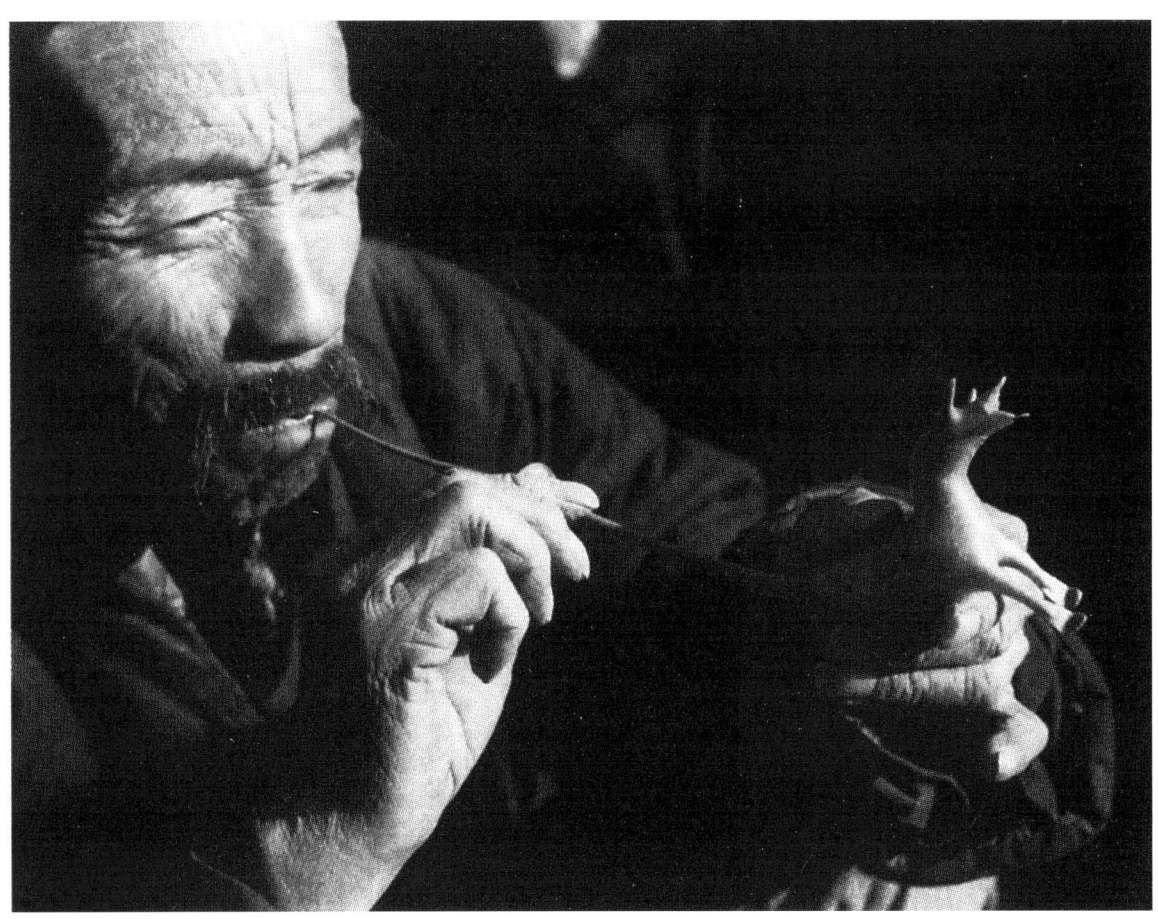

[德国] 赫达·莫里逊 [Germany] Hedda Morrison

吹糖人是一种民间手工艺，不仅出现在集市、庙会，小贩们也肩挑挑子走街串巷。挑子一头是带架的长方柜，柜子下面有一半圆形开口木圆笼，里面有一个小炭炉，炉上有一个小铁锅，中间放满了糖稀。吹糖人的小贩用拇指大小的一块糖稀，可以吹成各种各样的形状和造型。

As a form of folk art, blowing sugar figurines was not only seen at markets or temple fairs, but also in streets as performed by vendors who carried all the tools with a shoulder pole. On one side of the pole was a little cabinet set on a wooden cage with a charcoal stove inside. On the stove, a pot heated caramelized sugar. A sugar blower could make all kinds of figurines by blowing air into a small piece of sugar.

玩鹰的人
Men Playing with Hawks

［美国］西德尼·D·甘博 [America] Sidney D. Gamble

捕鹰、饲鹰、驯鹰、放鹰是清末民初北京一部分王公贵族、八旗子弟的嗜好，随着八旗子弟逐渐破落沦为一般市民，玩鹰这一活动也逐渐传到民众中，只是排场和玩法不同而已。

From the late Qing Dynasty (1644-1911) to the early Republic of China period (1912-1949), capturing, feeding, training and releasing hawks for hunting was a hobby for some aristocrats and descendants of the Eight Banner flag (military-administrative organizations of the Qing Dynasty) descendants. As the descendants became ordinary citizens, the activity of playing with hawks became popular among the general public. Compared with the previous trend, the difference was a lack of opulence and extravagance.

拉洋片
Performing a Slide-Show

[英国] 约翰·汤姆逊 [Britain] John Thomson

拉洋片是群众娱乐内容之一，清末民初流行于民间。一般是将彩色画片置于箱子里，箱子前装有放大镜的镜头。箱子边上有锣鼓架，用绳子和画片相连，拉动画片，随着敲击的锣鼓声，艺人唱起民间小调解说。

Performing slide-shows was a kind of entertainment very common at the turn from the late Qing Dynasty (1644-1911) to the Republic of China period (1912-1949). In such a show, colored pictures which were put into a box with a magnifying lens were linked with a gong-drum structure through a rope. While pulling the rope to change pictures and to ring the gong, a vendor told a story by singing a folk melody.

溜冰老人
An Ice-skating Senior

[德国] 赫达·莫里逊 [Germany] Hedda Morrison

溜冰是深受老北京人欢迎的一项闲暇运动。这位溜冰的老者常在北海展示技艺，他年轻的时候曾为慈禧太后表演过。

Ice-skating was a leisure activity popular among old Beijing citizens, like this grandpa who once performed for Empress Dowager Cixi when he was young. He often showcased his skills in Beihai Park.

北平第二届冰上运动大会
The Second Ice-Sports Competition in Peking

佚名 Unknown Photographer

清代，每年冬季在北京城内太液池（今北海）举办"冰嬉"活动，由内廷检阅八旗子弟兵。1915 年北京各公园对外开放后，北海、中南海和什刹海等处都设立冰场，群众自由参加冰上运动。20 世纪 20 年代西绅总会于冬季设临时的室内冰场，国外的冰上竞技运动技术和比赛方法自此传入北京。1937 年，北平市社会局在中南海举办第二届冰上运动大会。

In the Qing Dynasty (1644-1911), several "ice activities" were held at Taiyechi (now Beihai Park) in Beijing every winter. They were arranged for the royal court to review and inspect troops, which were descendants of the Eight Banner warriors. In 1915, since every park in Beijing was opened to the public, skating rinks were set up at Beihai, Zhongnanhai, Shichahai and other areas for people to participate in different kinds of on-ice activities. In the 1920s, Xi Shen International Club set up a temporary indoor skating rink for the winter, and the once foreign sport and its regulations were introduced to Beijing. In 1937, the Beiping Social Bureau held the Second Ice-Sports Competition in Zhongnanhai.

冬季储冰——打冰
Storing Ice in Winter-Breaking Ice

佚名 Unknown Photographer

北京人用冰的历史悠久。明清两代，皇宫把太液池的冰贮存在北海的冰窖里。清末以后，开始出现私营冰窖。民国三年（1914），政府规定冰窖开业只需向官方申请执照，再无其他限制。打冰时，先从极远的地方打起。冰块打出以后，用冰镩的倒须钩，将冰拉到冰面上，用大绳结鸳鸯扣套住冰块，由冰上一直拉到冰窖里。

Using ice in Beijing had a long history. In the Ming and Qing Dynasties (1368-1644, 1644-1911), the ice from Taiyechi was stored in an ice pit in Beihai Park according to the order of the royal court. After the late Qing Dynasty, private ice pits emerged. According to the rule of the government in the third year of the Republic of China (1914), ice pits could be operated by applying for a license, and were under no other restrictions. To break ice into pieces, one should start at the farthest place, pull the broken pieces onto the surface with iron hooks, tied them with ropes and pull them up to the ice pit.

交通运输

Traffic

人力车
Rickshaws

［德国］赫达·莫里逊 [Germany] Hedda Morrison

人力车，又称洋车或黄包车，是民国时期北京最普遍和廉价的交通工具。早期的人力车为宫廷使用，多用于太监执事们往返于紫禁城和颐和园之间。中国出现的第一辆人力车是1874年日本商人进献给慈禧太后的"铁皮车"，现陈列在颐和园中。袁世凯当政期间，曾在中南海组建了一支20人的人力车队，除供自家使用外也用于接送前来开会的北洋政府的官员。直到20世纪20年代，人力车才作为民间的代步工具广泛出现在北京的大街小巷。

Also called "foreign carts" or "yellow bag carts", rickshaws were the most common and cheapest means of transportation in Beijing during the period of the Republic of China (1912-1949). They were firstly used by the imperial court, mostly by eunuchs to shuttle between the Forbidden City and the Summer Palace. The first one in China, named a "sheet metal cart", was a present offered by a Japanese merchant in 1874 to the Empress Dowager Cixi, it's now displayed in the Summer Palace. When Yuan Shikai was in power in the period of the Republic of China, he once organized a motorcade of 20 rickshaws in Zhongnanhai, to serve his family and the officials of the Beiyang Government in Beijing for conferences. It was not until the 1920s when rickshaws became a popular means of transportation for common people in Beijing.

[德国] 海因茨·冯·佩克哈默 [Germany] Heinz v. Perckhammer

20世纪二三十年代，以经营性为目的的人力车市场发展迅速。车厂主要负责车辆的出租并定期向人力车夫收取"车份儿"，一般车厂还提供车辆维修服务，但是维修费用则要人力车夫自掏腰包。人力车拉客地点一般集中在戏园子、饭馆、火车站、澡堂子等地，以及东安市场、大栅栏、天桥等繁华商业区。从照片可见，当时为了便于对人力车进行有序的交通管理，很多地方都专门设有"停车处"。

The rickshaw taxi business began to prosper in the 1920s and 1930s with rickshaw owners leasing out rickshaws and collecting the rent. Some owners could also offer maintenance services, but at the expense of rickshaw-pullers. The drivers often went to theaters, restaurants, railway stations, public baths and busy shopping malls like the Dong'an market, Dashilan or Tianqiao market. The photo shows a "parking area" set for such vehicles in order to maintain traffic order.

王府井东堂前的人力车
Rickshaws before the East Cathedral at Wangfujing

[法国] 阿尔贝·杜帖特 [France] Albert Dutertre

坐落于王府井大街北段的天主教东堂地处繁华商业街区，堂外人力车随处可见。

In the bustling business area at the northern section of Wangfujing Street, where the East Cathedral was located, many rickshaws could be found.

金鱼胡同里的人力车
Rickshaws in Goldfish Lane

佚名 Unknown Photographer

骆驼队
A Camel Caravan

[美国] 赫伯特·C·怀特 [America] Herbert C. White

[英国] 唐纳德·曼尼 [Britain] Donald Mennie

唐代北京地区就已将骆驼广泛用作运输工具。北京地区骆驼最多的地方为京西门头沟、三家店到古城、八里庄一带，不少人家都养有骆驼，专门从事煤炭运输。民国时期，为了避免长长的驼队影响城市交通，对进城的骆驼队陆续有所限制。而后，随着汽车等交通工具的发展，骆驼作为交通运输工具逐渐被淘汰。

Since the Tang Dynasty (618-907), camels had been used as a means of transportation in the areas around Beijing, most prevalently in Mentougou, Sanjiadian to Gucheng and Balizhuang in the west of the city. The camels were raised in a large number, especially for supplying coals to the capital city. In the period of the Republic of China (1912-1949), camel caravans were restricted in the city due to worries that they would cause traffic jam. They were gradually replaced by automobiles when the latter became a major means of transportation.

[美国] 西德尼·D·甘博 [America] Sidney D. Gamble

[美国] 西德尼·D·甘博 [America] Sidney D. Gamble

交通运输　　　Traffic

出租马车
Horse-Drawn Carriages for Hire

佚名 Unknown Photographer

民国时期的载客马车从形制上有别于传统马车。民国初年，北京的街巷已经出现营业性的洋马车。当时马车行不但出租载客马车，同时还备有红白喜事所用的花车和素车。北京还成立了车业公会。后来由于汽车的兴盛，马车渐渐退出了历史舞台。

Horse-drawn carriages serving as taxis in the period of the Republic of China (1912-1949) were different in shape from traditional Chinese ones. When these foreign style vehicles were first put into operation in the early period of the Republic of China, taxi companies also offered fleet services for weddings and funerals in addition to leasing them. A carriage industry association was also founded in Beijing, but was bankrupt when automobiles were widely used instead of horse-drawn carriages.

送水车
A Water Wagon

旧时北京城内的饮用水主要来自胡同里的水井，井有井主。普通百姓可以免费自取井水，井主则靠雇人为富人家送水为生。

In the past, people in Beijing drank water from the wells inside alleyways. The owners of those wells allowed ordinary people to draw water by themselves for free, and made money by employing workers to deliver water to wealthy families.

[美国] 西德尼·D·甘博 [America] Sidney D. Gamble

运水
Carrying Water

[美国] 西德尼·D·甘博 [America] Sidney D. Gamble

山区小路上，一头小毛驴正在艰难地驮运四箱饮用水。

An exhausted donkey on a narrow mountain path was carrying four tanks of drinking water.

脚驴
Service Donkeys

[日本] 岩田秀则 [Japan] Hidenori Iwata

脚驴是指供人雇佣搬运或骑乘的驴。20世纪20年代以前，北京的交通极为不便，因而人们进城和城里人到郊区去大都雇佣毛驴以代步。雇佣毛驴有专门的驴市，俗称"驴口儿"。

Service donkeys carried cargos and were used for riding. Before the 1920s, due to the very inconvenient traffic in Beijing, people hired donkeys to go to the city or outskirts. They could also be leased in special donkey markets, called "Lv Kouer".

骡轿
A Mule-Carried Sedan Chair

[美国] 西德尼·D·甘博 [America] Sidney D. Gamble

骡车
A Mule Cart

佚名 Unknown Photographer

骡车是辛亥革命之前北京最主要的载人交通工具。因北京的骡车名冠北方各省，故有"京车"之称。骡车所用骡子大多来自陕西，以颈长、胸宽、腰瘦、胫细者为优。骡车分大鞍车、小鞍车，前者形体较大为王公贵族所使用，后者即普通轿车，如图。旧时北京的骡车除自用之外，还有营业性质的。骡车的经营者白天一般在胡同口、茶馆门前等待乘客租赁乘坐，因此有"站口儿"之说。

As the major means of transportation in Beijing before the Revolution of 1911, mule carts in Beijing were called "Capital Carts" because they were also popular in several provinces in Northern China. The best mules used in this service were mostly from Shanxi Province, featuring long necks, broad chests, slender waist and thin shins. Bigger carts were reserved for the nobility while smaller ones, like those in the photo, were used by the ordinary people. Their operators made money from them by waiting for customers in front of alleys or teahouses during the day.

[英国] 唐纳德·曼尼 [Britain] Donald Mennie

拉货大车
Big Cargo Carriages

[德国] 海因茨·冯·佩克哈默 [Germany] Heinz v. Perckhammer

大车在老北京的社会生活中扮演着重要角色。除乡村来的部分卖农产品的马车外，在前门、朝阳门、西直门等地还聚集上千辆专营运输的马车承揽各种短途零星货物运输。

Big cargo carriages played an important role of the social life in old Beijing. Besides those bringing agricultural products from villages, more than one thousand cargo carriages could be found making money in places like Qianmen, Chaoyangmen or Xizhimen by transporting all sorts of goods for a short distance.

[美国] 西德尼·D·甘博 [America] Sidney D. Gamble

[美国] 西德尼·D·甘博 [America] Sidney D. Gamble

乡下牛车
Bullock Carts

[美国] 西德尼·D·甘博 [America] Sidney D. Gamble

第一辆有轨电车
The First Tram

[美国] 西德尼·D·甘博 [America] Sidney D. Gamble

北京第一条有轨电车行驶线路为正阳门大街至西直门一线。当时，因为电车行进过程中会一直发出铃铛声提示行人注意安全，故老北京人又将其称为"diang diang 车"。照片为1924年第一辆有轨电车试运行时群众围观的热闹场景。

The first tram line in Beijing ran from Zhengyangmen Street to Xizhimen. Tramcars were also called "diang diang cars" by the old Beijing people due to their bell-ringing reminding passers-by to be cautious. The photo shows the applauding crowd celebrating the test of the first tram line in 1924.

京 华 旧 影
Old Photos of Beijing

天桥电车站
The Tianqiao Tram Station

佚名 Unknown Photographer

20世纪初，天津、上海、大连、广州等通商口岸先后出现了有轨电车。1921年北京官商合办在京成立了电车股份有限公司。1923年铺设路轨，1924年通车。当时北京有轨电车线路共6条。不同路线的站牌分别以红、黄、蓝、白、绿、黑六种颜色标识，以便乘车人辨识。

In the early 20th century, trams were put into operation in port cities like Tianjin, Shanghai, Dalian and Guangzhou. In 1921, a tram company was co-established by the government and merchants in Beijing. It laid railway tracks in 1923 and began to provide services in 1924. There were six lines at that time in Beijing, with signs in red, yellow, blue, white, green and black easier passengers to distinguish.

环城铁路德胜门车站
Deshengmen Station of the Loop Railway

同生照相馆 Tongsheng Photo Studio

1919 年，经过 5 年的建设，环城铁路东西两半段全线贯通。其路线与今天的北京地铁 2 号线大致相符。1959 年因新北京站开通，东便门至朝阳门站间线路拆除，1971 年 8 月为配合地铁的建设，环城铁路全部拆除。

In 1919, it took five years to finished the construction until the east and west sections of the loop Railwany in Beijing were linked. Its route was almost the same as that of present-day Beijing Subway Line 2. Due to the construction of a new Beijing Railway Station in 1959, the line between Dongbianmen and Chaoyangmen was demolished. The railway was removed completely in August 1971, for the construction of the subway.

东南角楼的环城铁路
The Loop Railway at the Southeastern Corner Tower

同生照相馆 Tongsheng Photo Studio

京 华 旧 影
Old Photos of Beijing

东北角楼的环城铁路
The Loop Railway at the Northeastern Corner Tower

同生照相馆 Tongsheng Photo Studio

前门火车站
Qianmen Railway Station

佚名 Unknown Photographer

前门火车站于光绪三十二年（1906）建成并使用，是我国铁路史上修建较早的火车站，也是当时中国最大的铁路交通枢纽。前门火车站在前门大街两侧分设东、西两站，分属不同的铁路局管辖。1949年以后，前门火车站成为主要客运站，改称北京站。1959年建成北京新站（即现北京站）。与此同时，前门火车站停止运营。20世纪60年代北京铁路局将其改建成北京铁路职工俱乐部、北京铁路文化宫。

Built and put into operation in the 32nd year of Guang Xu (1906) as one of the first stations in Chinese railway history, Qianmen Railway Station was the largest railway junction at that time in China. It was divided into two parts on the eastern and western side by Qianmen Street, and managed by two different railway bureaus. Serving as the main passenger station after 1949, Qianmen Railway Station was renamed Beijing Station. After a new station (the present-day Beijing Railway Station) was built in 1959, it quited operation. The station was then refurbished into a railway employee club and a cultural palace in the 1960s by the Beijing Railway Bureau.

[德国] 海因茨·冯·佩克哈默 [Germany] Heinz v. Perckhammer

交通运输　　Traffic

西直门火车站
Xizhimen Railway Station

同生照相馆 Tongsheng Photo Studio

西直门火车站即现在的北京北站，由中国著名的铁路工程师詹天佑设计和监造。1905年12月12日京张铁路西直门车站动工，1906年8月竣工。1909年北京丰台至张家口的京张线铁路通车，西直门车站正式投入运营。当时称作"京张铁路西直门车站"。1923年京张线铁路向西延伸至绥远，西直门车站改称平绥铁路西直门车站。如今在北京北站旧站房上写着"平绥铁路西直门车站"，1995年，北京市政府公布"平绥铁路西直门站旧址"为第五批北京市文物保护单位。

At the present-day Beijing North Station, Xizhimen Railway Station was designed by Zhan Tianyou, a famous railway engineer. Construction work began on December 12, 1905 and was finished in August of 1906. With the launching of the Beijing-Zhangjiakou Railway in 1909, it officially became operational. It was renamed Xizhimen Station of Pingsui Railway (Beijing-Suiyuan) in 1923, when the Beijing-Zhangjiakou Railway was extended westwards to Suiyuan. In 1995, the Beijing government designated it as one of the Fifth Batch of Municipal Cultural Heritage Sites.

青龙桥火车站
Qinglongqiao Railway Station

同生照相馆 Tongsheng Photo Studio

青龙桥火车站始建于 1905 年，是京张铁路线上著名的车站。京张铁路八达岭一线因地势陡峭，火车爬坡困难，在当时机械落后、资金短缺的情况下，詹天佑于青龙桥东沟设计"之"字形路线，通过借助大马力爬山机车掉头互相推挽的方式解决引力不足问题。这在中国铁路建造史上是一次独具匠心的精巧的设计。1922 年中华工程师学会在青龙桥火车站竖立了第一任会长詹天佑的铜像，总统徐世昌撰文并书写了纪念碑碑文。1982 年 5 月 20 日，詹天佑及夫人骨灰迁葬于此供世人凭吊。

Built in 1905, Qinglongqiao Railway Station was a famous station along the Jingzhang Railway. The Badaling section of the Jingzhang Railway was built in a mountainous area. To help trains climb over mountains with limited technology and funding, Zhan Tianyou designed a subtle zigzag railway line in the Qinglongqiao area. With strong powered locomotives pushing and pulling together at U-Turns, he solved the problem of insufficient traction. This very unique design in the Chinese history of railway construction demonstrated top engineering skills at the time. At the station in 1922, the Chinese Society of Engineers set a bronze statue of Zhan Tianyou, who was the first president of the organization. The text on the memorial monument was written by Xu Shichang, the President of the Republic of China. The bone ashes of Mr.Zhan and his wife were transferred to this place in 1982 for commemoration.

[德国] 海因茨·冯·佩克哈默 [Germany] Heinz v. Perckhammer

京奉铁路
Jingfeng Railway

[日本] 岩田秀则 [Japan] Hidenori Iwata

京奉铁路起自北京正阳门东车站，止于奉天（沈阳），是沟通北京与东北的重要交通干道。京奉铁路分段展筑而成，另建支线数条。其中1881年兴建的唐胥（唐山矿区至胥各庄）段长10公里，为中国第一条标准轨距铁路。1912年京奉铁路全线通车，初名京奉铁路，1928年改为北宁铁路。1949年后京奉铁路改为京沈铁路，现与沈哈铁路合称京哈铁路。

Jingfeng Railway, an important route linking Beijing and the Northeast, started in Beijing at Zhengyangmen East Station and ended in Fengtian (Shenyang). It was a combination of several sections and branch lines, among which, the 10 kilometers Tangxu section from the Tangshan mining area to Xugezhuang was finished in 1881 as the first one with a standard track gauge in China. Jingfeng Railway was renamed as Beining Railway in 1928, then Jingshen Railway in 1949, and eventually became part of the railway from Beijing to Harbin.

朝阳门内大街上的运粮车
Grain Carts on Chaoyangmen Inner Street

[法国] 斯提芬·帕瑟 [France] Stephane Passet

朝阳门是北京漕粮出入的城门。元、明、清时，京城粮食主要靠漕运，粮食来自南方产区，漕粮至通州，再经通惠河运至东便门大通桥码头，走陆路交通从朝阳门运入京城。故此，朝阳门内多粮仓，从现存地名亦可看出，如海运仓、禄米仓、北新仓等。

Chaoyangmen was the gate through which tribute rice was transported to Beijing. In the Yuan, Ming and Qing Dynasties (1271-1368, 1368-1644, 1644-1911), the grain for Beijing was mainly transported through the canal linking the capital and the rice Production areas in the south. The rice was transported first to Tongzhou, then through Tonghuihe to the Datongqiao port, from which it was delivered into the city by carts. Therefore, a lot of storehouses were built at the inner side of Chaoyangmen, such as Haiyuncang, Lumicang or Beixincang, the places which named after the storehouses.

运河
A Canal

[德国] 海因茨·冯·佩克哈默 [Germany] Heinz v. Perckhammer

通惠河历史悠久，建成至今已700多年，是北京城重要的漕运、排水河道。明清时期，江南漕运的粮食、物品均由大运河、通惠河水运到京。漕船行至通惠河距京城最近的码头大通桥止，其后货物转陆路进城。

With a long history of over 700 years, Tonghuihe had been an important watercourse for transportation and drainage in Beijing. In the Ming and Qing Dynasties (1368-1644,1644-1911), tribute rice and other goods were transported from south China to Beijing through the Grand Canal and Tonghuihe Arriving at Datongqiao, the closest pier to Beijing, the goods were unloaded and then transported on roads.

东便门外的运河码头
The Pier Outside Dongbianmen

[德国] 阿尔方斯．冯．穆默 [Germany] Alfons von Mumm

燃灯塔下的漕运码头
Water Transport Pier Under the Dipamkara Tower in Tongzhou

[英国] 费利斯·比托 [Britain] Felice Beato

主要摄影者简介

1. 奥斯瓦尔德·喜仁龙(1879-1966)，瑞典人。20世纪20年代初，曾在北京生活居住。他实地考察了北京当时遗存的城墙与城门，并于1924年在伦敦出版了《北京的城墙与城门》一书，书中包括细致的勘测观察手记、53幅城门建筑手绘图纸、128张实地拍摄的老城墙及城门的照片。

2. 海因茨·冯·佩克哈默(1895-1965)，德国人。在华期间，他拍摄了大量照片，影集在德国陆续出版，其代表作有《北京美观》、《百美影》等。

3. 唐纳德·曼尼(1876-1941)，英国人。他出版的第一本摄影画册是1920年的《北京美观》。该画册收录了66张作品，内容包括颐和园、北海、戒台寺等北京地区的风景名胜以及当时北京的市井生活场面。

4. 西德尼·戴维·甘博(1890-1968)，美国人。社会经济学家、摄影家。1908至1932年间甘博曾四次来华，旅居中国，其间拍摄了大量反映当时中国风貌的照片，总计5000余幅。

5. 小川一真(1860-1929)，日本人。1882年赴欧美等地学习摄影技术，归国后在东京开设照相馆"玉润馆"。1901年来到北京拍摄了诸多珍贵的影像资料，出版了《清国北京皇城写真贴》、《北清事变写真帖》等影集。

6. 山本赞七郎(1855—1943)，日本人。1882至1897年间在东京经营照相馆，后来到北京开设山本照相馆，曾为西太后等清政府贵族要员拍照，1911年回国。主要摄影作品为《北京名胜》。

7. 岩田秀则(1885-1962)，日本人。1906年1月来到北京，在山本照相馆担任摄影师，山本赞七郎回国后，岩田继续经营山本照相馆，二战后回国。主要摄影作品为《北京写真贴》。

8. 约翰·汤姆逊（1837-1921），英国人。从 1868 年开始了他的中国之旅，历时三年，拍摄了当时中国大部分地区的风光建筑、人物肖像、城市街头的生活。其作品《中国与中国人影像》，是世上首部用文字与图片合一的摄影集。

9. 赫达·莫里逊（1908-1991），德国人。1933 年来北京应聘担任德国人开设的哈同照相馆经理，历时 13 年。13 年中，她留下 5000 多张中国影像，10000 多张底片，28 个摄影集。其影集《洋镜头里的老北京》是 1933 至 1946 年间北京及市民生活的实录。

10. 赫伯特·C·怀特（1896-1962），美国人。1927 年，赫伯特·C·怀特主编的《燕京胜迹》，由上海商务印书馆出版，是一本制作考究的北京风景相册。

11. 儿岛鹭麿（生卒年不详），日本人。摄影师。主要摄影作品为 1909 年出版的《北清大观》。

12. 开发忍（生卒年不详），日本人。摄影师。主要摄影作品为 1939 年出版的《北京、天津大观》。

13. 不动健治（1898-1985），日本人。摄影师。曾在大阪经营艺术写真社，并发行《艺术写真》杂志，后作为同盟通信的随军记者来到中国拍摄了一系列的影像资料，主要作品为《北京与相机》等。

14. 阿尔方斯·冯·穆默（1859-？），德国人。1900 年 7 月来华，接任在义和团运动中被击毙的德国公使克林德。在华期间，他拍摄了大量反映庚子事变时期中国的政治、军事、名胜、民风等方面的照片，回国后，编辑出版了《德国公使照片日记》一书，成为其主要摄影作品。

15. 费利斯·比托（1832-1909），英国人。1860 年作为战地摄影记者随英法联军来到中国，是最早到中国拍摄照片的摄影师之一。比托拍摄了北京的城墙城门，烧毁前后的圆明园，还有幸成为了第一位拍摄中国皇室成员的外国摄影师，给恭亲王奕䜣拍摄了照片，被誉为"军事报道摄影的先驱者之一"。

Profile of Major Photographers

1. Osvald Siren (1879-1966), Swedish, lived in Beijing in the early 1920s. After a field inspection of the remains of city walls and gates of Beijing at that time, he published the book *The Walls and Gates of Peking*, which included detailed survey and observation notes, hand-drawn drawings of 53 gates and 128 photographs of walls and gates of the old city.

2. Heinz v. Perckhammer (1895-1965), German, took a large number of photographs during his stay in China. His albums were published in Germany successively with Peking, and *Edle Nacktheit in China* as his masterpieces.

3. Donald Mennie (1876-1941), British, published in 1920 his first photographic album *The Pageant of Peking* which contains 66 pieces of work, including the scenic spots of Beijing, like the Summer Palace, Beihai Park, Jietai Temple and others, and the life of ordinary residents in Beijing.

4. Sidney D. Gamble (1890-1968), an American social economist and photographer visited China four times and stayed here from 1908 to 1932. During his stay, he took more than 5,000 pieces of pictures reflecting the Chinese living style back then.

5. Kazuma Ogawa (1860-1929), Japanese, travelled to Europe and the United States in 1882 to learn photography technology before opening a photo studio "Yurun" in Tokyo. With the large number of valuable pictures he took after he came to Beijing in 1901, he published an albums *The Imperial City of Peking China, and the Souvenir of the Allies in North China*.

6. Sanshichiro Yamamoto (1855-1943), Japanese, ran a photo studio in Tokyo from 1882 to 1897, and later he came to Beijing and established his Yamamoto Photo Studio. He once served to take photos for Qing Dynasty's Empress Dowager Cixi and her high officials. He returned to Japan in 1911. His major work was Peking.

7. Hidenori Iwata (1885-1962), Japanese, came to Beijing to work at the Yamamoto Photo Studio in January of 1906. After Sanshichiro Yamamoto returned to Japan, he continued to operate the Studio and returned to Japan after World War II. His main work was the *Photographic Album Peking.*

8. John Thomson (1837-1921), British, began his three-year journey in China from 1868, during which, he photographed architecture, persons and urban life in most parts of China. His work the *Ill ustrations of China and its People* was the first collection with a combination of photos and pictures worldwide.

9. Hedda Morrison (1908-1991), German, came to Beijing in 1933 as the photo manager of the Hatong Photo Studio opened by the Germans for 13 years. During those years, she recorded more than 5,000 pieces of Chinese images, leaving more than 10,000 negatives and 28 photo collections, with the album *A Photographer in Old Peking* as an real-time record of this city and its citizens' life from 1933 to 1946.

10. Herbert C. White (1896-1962), American, served as the editor-in-chief of the *Peking the Beautiful*, which was published by the Shanghai Commercial Press in 1927. It is a photo album of Beijing landscape which is delicately made.

11. Sagimaro Kojima (with birth and death years unknown), Japanese, was a photographer whose major photographic work was the *View and Custom of North China* published in 1909.

12. Shinobu Kaihatsu (with birth and death years unknown), was a Japanese photographer whose major photographic work was *the Grand View of Beijing and Tianjin* published in 1939.

13. Kenji Fudou (1898-1985), Japanese, operated an art photo studio in Osaka and published a Magazine called *the Art Photo*. He took a large number of videos and pictures after he came to China as an army reporter. His main works were *Beijing and Camera.*

14. Alfons von Mumm (1859-?), a German photographer, came to China to serve as the successor of Ketteler, the former German Minister Counselor who was shot dead during the Yihetuan uprising. During his stay in China, he took a large number of photographs reflecting China's politics, military affairs, places of interest and folk customs during the Boxer Rebellion. After returning Germany, he edited and published a book entitled *A Diary in Pictures*.

15. Felice Beato (1832-1909), a British battlefield photographer, came to China in 1860 with the British and French forces. As one of the first photographers who came to China, he shot pictures of walls and gates of Beijing, and in particular the Winter Palace before and after it was burnt down. Fortunate enough to be the first foreigner who took pictures for the member of the royal family, he recorded Prince Yi Xin and was honored as "one of the pioneers in military reportage photography".

后 记

　　历经百年沧桑的首都图书馆有着一个独特的馆藏体系，那就是汇聚了诸多北京地方文献资源的专藏。1958年，北京地方文献中心成立，经过60年的建设与发展，不断积累和丰富着这座研究级的宝库，使之一枝独秀，为世人所瞩目，特别是不同历史时期的图片资料备受社会和业内的关注。2007年，我们建立了自己的网站——"北京记忆"大型多媒体数据库，全面向社会展示北京文献，引发人们对北京记忆的研究与探讨，2017年，我们对网站进行了全新改版和升级，更加注重北京传统文化的传播与读者的互动。让北京这座城市在日新月异的发展过程中，逝去的影像依旧存留在人们的记忆中。这是北京人共有的记忆，也是世界文化的记忆，北京地方文献工作者萌发了一个留住记忆影像的念头——精选和编辑旧京影像，为此我们推出了《京华旧影》图集。

　　《京华旧影》在编选上分为内容和时间两条主线：内容上侧重城市风貌和百姓生活；时间上以清末民国为主体。参照这两条主线，我们在大量的老照片中精挑细选，仔细斟酌，最终形成定稿。力求反映那个时期的北京风貌，体现当时北京百姓的生活场景。

　　《京华旧影》收录的老照片尽可能地考证了摄影者的国籍和姓名，并加以标注，部分不清楚摄影者的图片标注为佚名，以此表示尊重前人的工作成果和知识产权，并在此向所有的拍摄者表示最诚挚的感谢和敬意！

　　影像的记忆最能打动人心，愿我们编辑的这些记忆影像能够唤起读者对北京记忆的更大热情，和我们一起，共同构建一个完整的"北京记忆"。

Postscript

There is a special collection system in the time-honored Capital Library of China. That is the special collection of many local Beijing literature and archival resources. After 60 years of construction and development since 1958 when the Local Literature Center of Beijing, its predecessor, was established, the library keeps enriching its unique and splendid collections, especially famous for its photos at different historical periods. In 2007, "Beijing Memory", our website and a big multimedia database was set up, showcasing Beijing literature and archives to the public, generating the study and discussion of our past. In 2017, the website was upgraded with more focus on the traditional culture of the city and more interaction with readers. As the capital city changes with each passing day, some old images are still in the memory of residents who are willing to share this memory with other people in Beijing and those around the world. So an idea occurred to the employees at the Local Beijing Literature Center, that is, to choose and edit the old photos of Beijing, and to publish an album so as to keep the memory alive.

Content and time are the two principal themes of the album with a focus on the image of the city and the life of Beijingers in history, particularly during the periods of the late Qing Dynasty (1644-1911) and the Republic of China (1911-1949). Photos are chosen, then screened again and again based on these two criteria to reflect the real image of Beijing and the everyday life of citizens at the time.

Editors have tried their best to identify the nationalities and names of photographers who shot the photos collected in the album and include the information herein. For the photos whose photographers cannot be identified, the word "an unknown photographer" was used to show the sincerest gratitude and tribute to the photographers, respect for their work, and intellectual property rights.

As memory from images touches people the most, we hope that the photos herein will incite the readers' passion toward the memory of old Beijing so that they can join us in making the memory completely.